THE VIKING WAY

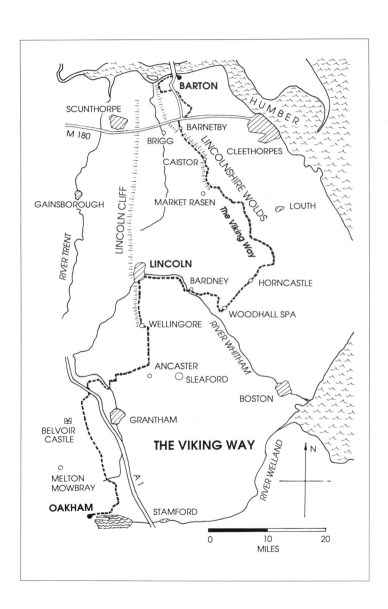

SCUNTHORPE

BARTON

HUMBER

M 180

BARNETBY

BRIGG

CLEETHORPES

CAISTOR

LINCOLNSHIRE WOLDS

GAINSBOROUGH

MARKET RASEN

LOUTH

LINCOLN CLIFF

RIVER TRENT

The Viking Way

LINCOLN

BARDNEY

HORNCASTLE

WOODHALL SPA

WELLINGORE

RIVER WITHAM

ANCASTER

SLEAFORD

BOSTON

BELVOIR CASTLE

GRANTHAM

THE VIKING WAY

N

MELTON MOWBRAY

A 1

RIVER WELLAND

OAKHAM

STAMFORD

0   10   20

MILES

THE VIKING WAY

BY

JOHN STEAD

Maps and line drawings by Don Cameron

CICERONE PRESS MILNTHORPE CUMBRIA

"On either side of the river lie,
Long fields of barley and of rye,
That clothe the wold and meet the sky"
Alfred (Lord) Tennyson
The Lady of Shalott

* * *

* * *

Acknowledgements

I would particularly like to thank those people who offered information and advice during research for this guide, which has been gratefully used. Special thanks are due to Don Cameron for the excellent sketches and strip maps. I would also like to thank all of my friends, without whom very little would have been possible.

* * *

This book is dedicated to all those who walk the Viking Way.

CONTENTS

		Distance	Page
Introduction			6

The Lincolnshire Wolds

Chapter 1:	Barton upon Humber to Barnetby	12 miles	17
Chapter 2:	Barnetby to Caistor	8 miles	30
Chapter 3:	Caistor to Ludford	12 miles	41
Chapter 4:	Ludford to Scamblesby	11 miles	55
Chapter 5:	Scamblesby to Horncastle	8 miles	63

Central Lincolnshire

Chapter 6:	Horncastle to Woodhall Spa	6 miles	75
Chapter 7:	Woodhall Spa to Lincoln	16 miles	84
Chapter 8:	The City of Lincoln		93
Chapter 9:	Lincoln to Wellingore	10 miles	104

South Lincolnshire and Rutland

Chapter 10:	Wellingore to Carlton Scroop	10 miles	111
Chapter 11:	Carlton Scroop to Woolsthorpe	15 miles	121
Chapter 12:	Woolsthorpe to Sewstern	8 miles	137
Chapter 13:	Sewstern to Oakham	14 miles	143
Chapter 14:	Stamford		156

Total Walking Distance: 130 miles

Introduction

The Viking Way runs for 130 miles between Barton upon Humber and Oakham, passing through some of the quietest and most attractive scenery in eastern England. The passage from Tennyson quoted at the front of the book is perhaps slightly misleading since the poem goes on to describe the *Camelot* of Arthurian legend. However it does express something of the landscape you might expect to see, and Tennyson was no stranger to these parts. The idea of a long distance path through Lincolnshire was fostered by John Hedley Lewis, a keen rambler and former Chairman of the County Council who died in 1976. The following year the Viking Way was drawn up by the County of Lincolnshire in association with the neighbouring counties of Humberside and Leicestershire.

The Ramblers' Association was also consulted over the definition of the route, and in places local groups have assisted with waymarking and path clearance. The Way has existed for many years as a recognisable long distance footpath. Only recently has it been considered by the Countryside Commission (along with nine other possible routes) for designation as a new 'national' trail, although no firm proposals exist as yet.

Leaving Barton upon Humber close by the impressive structure of the Humber Bridge, the Way heads S along the line of the Lincolnshire Wolds, running close to the W scarp edge in places and elsewhere further E amongst the rolling hills. Here the path skirts past several deserted medieval village sites, visible as ridges and hollows in the adjacent fields.

After 50 miles the Way reaches the old market town of Horncastle, and then turns SW to follow the course of an old railway track to Woodhall Spa. From here it heads NW through the low-lying valley of the River Witham, then along the edge of the fens to the City of Lincoln with its wealth of historic buildings, museums, archaeological remains and its crowning glory the magnificent, medieval Cathedral.

From Lincoln the route turns S following the Jurassic escarpment (known as 'the cliff'), running along the edge the plateau for several miles. Before long it reaches the line of Roman Ermine Street, part of which runs as an open green lane. The Way then diverts SW along footpaths towards Marston and Woolsthorpe. Thus it avoids Grantham which is, nevertheless, a good access point for the S part of the Way with some interesting historic attractions in the vicinity. Near Woolsthorpe and just over the boundary into Leicestershire is the splendidly restored Belvoir Castle, well worth a visit.

The Way now resumes a S course along the county boundary with Leicestershire, following an ancient trackway known as Sewstern Lane. This continues for several miles down to the village of the same name. The footpath finally reaches the broad expanse of Rutland Water, the largest reservoir in southern England, and heads along its N shore to Oakham, the historic centre of Rutland.

On the Way you will come across many interesting parish churches and many of these are described in some detail. Also within reach of the path there are abbeys, castles and prehistoric sites which will reward a brief detour. Such places include Thornton Abbey (near Barton), Tattershall Castle (near Woodhall Spa) and Belvoir Castle (near Woolsthorpe). These are described at the end of the appropriate chapter, with brief details on admission and times of opening. Lincoln and Stamford are described in separate chapters, and there are special sections on other historic towns such as Horncastle, Woodhall Spa and Grantham.

This landscape has literary connections with Alfred (Lord) Tennyson at Somersby (Chapter 5 includes a short biography); with George Crabbe, the 18th Century Suffolk poet and one time domestic chaplain at Belvoir Castle; and with John Clare, the farm labourer-poet who lived for much of his life in the vicinity of Stamford. William Cobbett, the inveterate traveller and polemicist, also passed through the area in 1830 on the East Midlands stages of his *Rural Rides*.

Walking the Viking Way

The guide is arranged in three sections corresponding to the broad geographical divisions traversed by the route. These are the Lincolnshire Wolds, central Lincolnshire (including the Witham plain and Lincoln 'cliff'), and south Lincolnshire and Rutland (the latter now incorporated within Leicestershire). In short the path runs 51 miles S from Barton, then 22 miles NW to Lincoln, followed by a further 57 miles S to Oakham. In keeping with its official designation I have chosen to describe the route running north to south, but there is no special reason why it should not be walked in the other direction.

Each chapter describes a section of path normally covering no more than 12 miles, with three slightly longer stretches. At the moment many locals walk the path in daily stages, but there is an increasing trend for the entire route to be tackled as a long distance footpath. With no special effort this should be accomplished easily in the space of a fortnight. Some of the most attractive scenery is found in the Wolds, a designated Area of Outstanding Natural Beauty, although the strange, wilderness-like quality of the plateau lands S of Lincoln and the quiet isolation of Sewstern Lane should not be underestimated.

The strip maps in this guide are drawn at a scale of 1:50,000 and show details of the path, plus local villages and landmarks. Hopefully these are sufficiently accurate to follow the route but they are best used in conjunction with the relevant Ordnance Survey maps (see Maps). Nearly all of the Viking Way is very well-defined with good waymarks: for this the respective county authorities are to be congratulated, but neither should we forget those farmers and land-owners who have made a special effort to define the route, sometimes by leaving a wide stretch of unploughed land at the edge of a field.

The Way often runs as a green path along a field's edge, sometimes as a double track or green lane. In Lincolnshire, waymarks are indicated by the distinctive Viking helmet symbol; in Leicestershire by the slight variant of a Viking helmet and shield. Most public stretches of the path are mown regularly in season, although in places it may become slightly overgrown (comments on the state of the path should be directed to the county authorities listed at the end of the Introduction).

In places local buses and trains are available, and brief details of services are included at the end of each chapter. A useful means of getting around is the *East Midlands Railrover* which covers the whole area, with access to towns and cities including Barton, Lincoln, Grantham, Stamford and Oakham (available from all major BR stations in the East Midlands).

There is a fairly good range of accommodation close to the path, including many inns and guest-houses. Some of these may require a short detour on foot. An alternative is to stay in one of the larger towns within reach of the Way. Campsites are in reasonable supply (especially in the Lincolnshire Wolds) and many sites also accept caravans. In addition to those sites listed there are a number of members-only sites certificated by the Caravan Club.

It is possible to cycle certain parts of the route: 5 miles along the old railway track between Horncastle and Woodhall Spa, a 6¹/₂ mile stretch of Ermine Street S of Lincoln and 8 miles along Sewstern Lane S of Woolsthorpe. None of these are dedicated cycle routes, so mountain bikes may be the best option to cope with the uneven surface (especially along Sewstern Lane). Cycling, however, is a very effective means of getting around and it would enable you to combine stretches of the path with a tour of the area - and the chance to visit historic sites such as Tattershall Castle.

Geology and Scenery
In geological terms this part of eastern England consists very largely of sedimentary deposits from the Jurassic and Cretaceous periods. These form a series of plateau ridges interspersed with clay lowlands. In general the rocks are tilted E at a shallow angle, producing scenery which is fairly gentle, if not as flat as sometimes imagined.

The Jurassic ridgeline of Northamptonshire extends N into Rutland and Lincolnshire, forming the plateau of Middle and Upper Lias clays crossed by Sewstern Lane. Thereafter the ridge turns NW past Grantham and N again to form the scarp face of Lincoln 'cliff'. The topmost deposits of the ridge are of good quality Lincolnshire limestone, quarried in various locations (the famous Ancaster stone for example).

Lincoln 'cliff' is a continuous feature for 50 miles from Ancaster to the Humber, passing through Lincoln itself and giving rise to the prominent N side hill on which the Cathedral stands. Elsewhere the Lower Lias clays contain bands of ironstone, once mined extensively in the vicinity of Scunthorpe and further S near Woolsthorpe. Further E there is a succession into the Upper Jurassic series, forming the clay lowlands of the lower Witham and Ancholme river valleys. In both cases these are overlain by Quaternary deposits (alluvium, glacial tills and fen peat in the lower Witham Valley).

The pronounced W ridge of the Lincolnshire Wolds is formed by basal clays and sandstones, including greensand in the S Wolds, with outcrops of Claxby ironstone further N. Such local outcrops are very much reflected in the choice of building materials for the parish churches. The transition to rocks of the Cretaceous period becomes complete in the ridges of the higher Wolds, which consist wholly of chalk (sometimes overlain with glacial tills). The ridges extend N-S, often for many miles, and are nowadays intensively cultivated for cereals.

East of the Wolds the Cretaceous rocks dip gradually beneath the Quaternary deposits of the costal plain (part of the shoreline continues to extend itself seawards at the expense of eroded stretches of North Humberside). Further S is the vast expanse of fenland towards Boston and the Wash.

History of the Viking Danelaw

For centuries Lincolnshire has been a vast rural area notable for the quality of its soils, and the richness and diversity of its agriculture. Prior to the Middle Ages, however, much of the land probably remained as forest or marshy fen. The Romans imposed a sense of order with the construction of roads and new settlements, while Lincoln soon assumed a special importance as a fortified city.

The Anglo-Saxon invasions of the 5th and 6th centuries heralded a new era in which the land was divided between the Kingdom of Lindsey (with Lincoln retained as the capital) and parts of North Anglia. The Saxons were essentially farmers, and having driven out or subdued Romano-British forces, they proceeded to settle down and cultivate the land. Most agricultural settlements were probably of timber and thatch, which perhaps explains the lack of visible remains. Important burial grounds have, however, been discovered at Barton upon Humber and Lovedon Hill. Later the Saxons built churches of stone according to simple designs (notable examples have survived at Barton and in Lincoln itself).

Whilst England remained divided between a number of Saxon kingdoms, the Middle Saxon period of the 8th century established a relative peace. This was rudely shattered by Viking raids, first at Lindisfarne in 793 AD, then at many other monasteries further south. To the undefended religious houses these raids came as a complete surprise and were nothing short of devastating.

Sporadic raids continued until the Danes attacked in successive waves between 865-880 AD, gaining control of parts of Northumbria, Lindsey and East Anglia. Contemporary Anglo-Saxon chroniclers attest to the ferocity of these attacks which were accompanied with much destruction and burning. At first the invaders marched hither and thither in search of conquest: York fell in 867 and in 870 the Danes moved W to threaten Wessex under Alfred, but after several battles they withdrew to London. In 874 the Kingdom of Mercia fell and a second assault was launched on Wessex although it was not until 878 that the Danes, now under Guthrum, looked set to overwhelm Alfred's forces.

The Danes advanced from Gloucester to Chippenham, whilst a sea-bourne force attacked the coast of Devon. Quite undeterred by this, Alfred built a fortress at Athelney on the Somerset levels, and uniting the remaining Wessex armies in S England, he advanced to Edington and scored an emphatic victory. Following his defeat Guthrum was received by Alfred and baptized as a Christian, before withdrawing with his troops to East Anglia.

Not content with this, Alfred then proceeded to fortify many of the southern English towns and in 886 he occupied London. At the same time a further treaty was struck with Guthrum, recognising Alfred as the English leader and defining Guthrum's kingdom E of the River Lea and Watling Street. The area now occupied by the Danes became known as *Danelaw*, and was dominated by the 'five boroughs' - Nottingham, Lincoln, Stamford, Derby and Leicester. Owing to the lack of written history we have virtually no records of life under Danish rule, but the situation thus established prevailed until after Alfred's death in 899.

Alfred was succeeded by his son, Edward the Elder, who forged a new alliance with his sister, Aethelflaed of Mercia. The two of them then mounted a remarkable campaign of re-conquest which over the next 20 years saw the Danish frontier progressively driven backwards. In 910 the Danes were defeated at Tettenhall in Staffordshire, and by 917 the whole of East Anglia was once again under English control. Edward continued his military campaigns, while Aethelflaed rebuilt fortifications at Chester and Runcorn against the threat of Norse attack from the NW.

By 920 AD the English frontier had reached a line joining the Humber and Mersey. On the death of Aethelflaed, Edward was recognised as King of England and in a treaty signed at Bakewell received submissions from Constantine the King of the Scots, Raegnald of York and other Northumbrian leaders. The English success story continued over several decades with the recapture of Northumbria and in 954 the final expulsion of the Norse ruler, Eric Bloodaxe, from York. This, however, was not the end of the story for it presaged the emergence of new and highly trained professional armies in Denmark under the aegis of the *Jomsvikings*.

During the reign of the aptly named Aethelred the Unready (978-1013), Viking raids began again with renewed vigour. In a half-hearted attempt to prevent them, the English King and noblemen were forced into parting with vast quantities of gold and silver coin which was known as *Danegeld*. The warrior bands from Scandinavia soon realised they were on to a good thing, and over successive years the amount paid in Danegeld increased dramatically, reaching the then staggering sum of £36,000 in 1007.

A particularly fierce series of raids took place between 1009-1012, involving several battles and the exaction of further tributes. This culminated in the murder of the Archbishop of Canterbury, an event so gruesome that even the Viking leader, Thorkell the Tall, was prompted to change sides (only to change back again after the fall of Aethelred). In the final chapter of this sorry tale Swein Forkbeard, the King of the Danes, entered the mouth of the Humber in 1013 and sailed up to Gainsborough, from where he conducted yet more raids into the heart of England. When London surrendered Aethelred fled to Normandy and Swein was promptly declared King of England. Soon afterwards he died, to be replaced by Cnut who ruled until 1035.

This period was something of a respite from continuous warring, and for the first time the whole of England was united under a Danish king. Cnut retained his hold over the Danish throne and at one time even extended his empire to cover Norway and modern-day Sweden. In England he is best remembered for the incident in which he stood on the shore of an Essex creek and commanded the tide to stay down. Soon afterwards of course he got his feet wet, leading some to suppose he was rather simple-minded. In fact Cnut was said to have used this event to demonstrate to his assembled thanes the humility of kings and the hopelessness of denying the natural forces of God's earth!

After the Battle of Hastings in 1066 it took William the Conquerer around five years to suppress most of the resistance to Norman rule. Parts of the country (especially latter-day Yorkshire) were laid waste in order to forestall any insurgence, but in a spirit of defiance Hereward the Wake (sometimes called 'the last of the Saxons') led a series of revolts in East Anglia and the Midlands. Having formed a temporary alliance with a Danish force in 1069, he conducted a successful raid on Peterborough whilst the Danes occupied Ely. The rebellion was short-lived, however, for in the following year William made his own treaty with the Danes and most of Hereward's forces surrendered at Ely.

Despite leaving little in the way of permanent remains, the Danish and other Viking settlers established a Scandinavian influence which is most obvious in place names to this day. Within the area once ruled as Danelaw there is a proliferation of town and village names with the suffix 'by' (meaning place), such as Grimsby, Barnetby and Normanby. Others include 'thorpe' (meaning small village), surviving as Scunthorpe, Cleethorpes and Woolsthorpe. The Scandinavian 'kirk' for church is also represented in Kirton and Kirkstead. The Viking Way (which might otherwise be called the Lincolnshire Way) traverses through the heart of the old Danelaw area and therefore has a just claim to its name.

The Scandinavian influence was, however, more than just linguistic. After the invasions of the 9th century the Danelaw became an area which was governed literally according to Scandinavian custom and practice. England's King Edgar declared in 962 that the Danes could exercise their own rights "according to the good laws they can best decide on." Later we learn from the Wantage Code (issued during the reign of Aethelred) that the leading thanes in each Wapentake could act as a legal jury in all cases of civil wrong. Scandinavian currencies were also issued from the mints at Lincoln, Stamford and York.

Perhaps the most fascinating distinction was found in the area of land tenure. Wheras Anglo-Saxon society displayed many of the characteristics of an emerging feudal order, the Danelaw was dominated by Freemen or Sokemen. Such farmers held the status of tenants but were not bound by the requirements of servile duty towards the landlords. The difference between Freemen and Sokemen hinged around a precise legal definition of the landlord-tenant relationship. There was a clear contrast, however, with the Saxon *ceorls* (churls), a group which later re-emerged as the villeins or bound peasants of medieval England. During the Danish occupation over fifty per cent of the population in the Lincolnshire area was said to consist of Sokeman families.

Another difference was the relatively weak and impoverished nature of the Church, which at that time was unable to accumulate large holdings of wealth. Only after the Norman Conquest did the position change as Cistercian and other monastic houses moved into the area and received grants of land from the King.

Further Reading

The Vikings in Britain , H R Lyon, Book Club Associates (1977).

An Introduction to Anglo-Saxon England, Peter Hunter-Blair, CUP (1956).

A Guide to Anglo-Saxon Sites, Nigel and Mary Kerr, Granada (1982).

The Making of the English Landscape, W G Hoskins, Hodder and Stroughton (1988).

The Lost Villages of England, M W Beresford, Lutterworth (1954).

Rural Rides, William Cobbett, P Davies (1930).

Lincolnshire (The Buildings of England), Sir Nikolaus Pevsner, Penguin (1964)

Leicestershire (The Buildings of England), Pevsner, 2nd Edition by Elizabeth Williamson, Penguin (1984).

A Portrait of Lincolnshire, Michael Lloyd, Robert Hale (1983).

Lincolnshire and South Humberside, David Kaye, Shire (1984).

Journey Home, John Hillaby, Constable (1983).

A Tennyson Companion, F B Pinion, Macmillan (1984).

John Clare - The Rural Muse, Carcanet New Press (1982).

British Regional Geology - Eastern England, HMSO (1980).

Maps

The Viking Way is marked on all the relevant OS 1:50,000 maps. The following should be quite sufficient for walking the route if used in conjunction with the strip maps in this guide:

Sheet 112 Scunthorpe	(Barton - Grasby)
Sheet 113 Grimsby and Cleethorpes	(Grasby - Burgh on Bain)
Sheet 122 Skegness	(Burgh on Bain -Woodhall Spa)
Sheet 121 Lincoln	(Woodhall Spa - Byard's Leap)
Sheet 130 Grantham	(Byard's Leap - Exton)
Sheet 141 Kettering and Corby	(Exton - Oakham)

For those who would prefer to follow the route in more detail the following 1:25,000 sheets are also available:

Sheet 696   Kingston upon Hull (South)
Sheet 719   Brigg and Caistor
Sheet 707   Immingham and Elsham
Sheet 730   South Kelsey and Tealby
Sheet 747   Market Rasen
Sheet 748   Louth
Sheet 766   Tetford and Baumber
Sheet 783   Horncastle
Sheet 782   Metheringham and Woodhall Spa
Sheet 765   Wragby
Sheet 764   Lincoln and Saxilby
Sheet 781   Lincoln South
Sheet 797   Newark on Trent and Navemby
Sheet 814   Long Bennington and Caythorpe
Sheet 835   Grantham and Belvoir
Sheet 855   Colsterworth and Waltham
Sheet 876   Wymondham and Cottesmore
Sheet 896   Rutland Water

Comments on waymarking and the condition of the path should be addressed to the appropriate county authority:-

Barton upon Humber to Bigby:

> Director of Technical Services,
> Humberside County Council,
> County Hall,
> Beverley, North Humberside.

Bigby to Woolsthorpe:

> Director of Recreational Services,
> Lincolnshire County Council,
> County Offices,
> Newland,
> Lincoln.

Woolsthorpe to Oakham:

> Director of Planning and Transportation,
> Leicestershire County Council,
> County Hall,
> Glenfield,
> Leicester.

Humber Bridge

CHAPTER 1
Barton upon Humber to Barnetby

Barton upon Humber (See map p18)
Barton is a small town (population 9,000) situated near the southern
end of the Humber Bridge. Its history stretches back as far as
Romano-British times and it was recorded as a ferry and market town
in the Domesday Book of 1086. Later it was eclipsed as a port by the
development of Hull.

In some ways time has passed Barton upon Humber by, but it
retains a certain historic charm. The streets are full of attractive, brick-
built houses from the 18th and 19th centuries and there are no less
than 177 buildings listed as of historic or architectural interest. The
Town Trail (leaflet available at the museum) takes around two to
three hours to complete. Despite the closure of the New Holland ferry
in 1978, the rail service from Grimsby has survived (though its future
may be doubtful). The Humber Link bus service departs from the
station concourse, providing a connection to Hull across the Humber
Bridge.

History of the Town
Barton was probably established as a settlement during Roman
times, but in the 5th century AD the British garrison was withdrawn
to protect Rome from pagan attack. As a result, Germanic mercenar-
ies were used to defend parts of eastern England, a fact confirmed by
the discovery of early Germanic cemeteries on Humberside. In the
6th and 7th centuries the Anglo-Saxon invasions began in earnest
with the settlers occupying farmland and spreading the Saxon influence (seen in place names, including 'Barton') throughout the countryside. A pagan Anglian cemetery from this period has been excavated in the vicinity of Tower Mill.

South Humberside became part of the ancient Kingdom of Lindsey, later incorporated within Mercia. The growing influence of
Christianity saw most of the Saxon tribes converted by the end of the
7th century. In 667 AD Bede records that King Wulfhere of Mercia

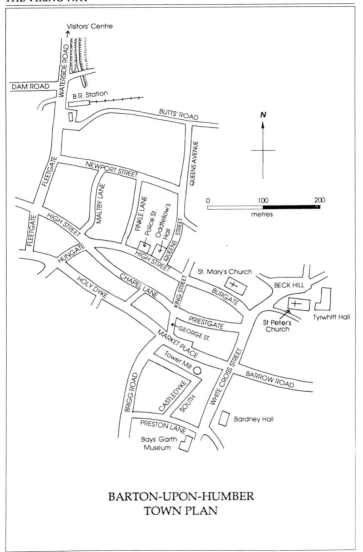

BARTON-UPON-HUMBER
TOWN PLAN

gave fifty hides of land* at nearby **Barrow on Humber** to build a monastery. The monastery was founded by St Chad, then Bishop of Mercia, but was later destroyed by Viking raids in the 9th century.

Barton developed as a port during medieval times, with an active trade in wool, fish, leather and wine. Nevertheless it was soon overshadowed by Kingston upon Hull, which was granted a Royal Charter by Edward I in 1299. In the 17th century religious intolerance under James I made life difficult or dangerous for early non-conformists and in 1609 groups of these 'Independants' sailed from Immingham Creek for the safety of Holland, though not before a number had been arrested. Later, in 1620, they reformed as the 'Pilgrim Fathers', sailing from Plymouth en route for Massachusetts.

Among 19th century travellers, William Cobbett visited Barton in April 1830 on the East Midlands stage of his *Rural Rides*. Having travelled from Boston and Horncastle, he continued over the E side of the Lincolnshire Wolds, arriving in Barton on April 15th. From here he crossed the Humber in a 'steam boat' to Hull, returning a few days later on the return journey to Lincoln.

Barton remains a quiet town to this day, though it hardly deserved Defoe's famous remark that it was "A town noted for nothing that I know of, but an ill-favoured dangerous passage or ferry, over the Humber to Hull."

Ferry crossings over the Humber have a history of turbulent waters, swirling currents and difficult mudbanks. On occasions rolling sea fogs also caused delays, sometimes for several hours. In 1948 the paddle-steamer *Tattershall Castle* became the first such vessel to be fitted with radar, providing a distinct advantage over its sister ship, the *Lincoln Castle*. The latter remained in service on the New Holland-Hull route until 1978, carrying up to nine hundred passengers and twenty vehicles, though drawing only 4 feet 6 inches of water. The ship has now been restored in Grimsby dock as a tourist attraction.

The **Humber Bridge** was officially opened by the Queen on July 17th 1982, after nearly ten years in construction at a cost of £91 million. Thus the ancient barrier was finally overcome and North and South

---

* A hide of land is a variable amount but generally assumed to be enough land to support a family and its dependents, thought to be about 120 acres.

Humberside were connected by the longest single-span suspension bridge in the world. At 4,626 feet the central span comfortably out-distances the next longest (across the Verrazano Narrows in New York) by some 400 feet. Despite uncertain predictions, it is now said to carry over three million vehicles per year. On either side of the carriageways there are wide cycle and footways. Hessle on the N shore is the start of the **Wolds Way**, so the Humber Bridge provides a useful link.

A Tour of the Town (See map p18)

From the railway station, go down ancient Fleetgate for 200 yards, passing the Steam Packet pub on the R, and turn L along the High Street. This is one of the most attractive streets in Barton, with many 18th century buildings and is reminiscent of coaching towns in the south of England. At Junction Square take the L fork and continue along High Street and then onto Burgate, passing the mid 19th century police station on the L.

After about 100 yards you will reach **St Mary's Church** on the L. Built as a replacement for the earlier Saxon church, St Mary's was completed between the 12th and 15th centuries. The interior is high, wide and spacious, possibly an indication of medieval prosperity. The chancel floor has a brass dedicated to Simon Seman, a 15th century London wine merchant who died here.

On leaving the church continue to the end of Burgate, then turn L onto Beck Hill. After a few yards **St Peter's Church** is revealed on the opposite side. This is considered to be one of the finest remaining late Saxon churches in the country, now extensively restored as a monu-ment by English Heritage. The 10th century tower is plainly built with decorative stone strips (or pilasters), a clear indication of Saxon work. The main body of the church is of the 12th-13th centuries and there is a fine 15th century rood screen. Perhaps the most fascinating item is the incised head over the chancel arch, most likely of 10th century origin and thought to represent the face of Christ. Recent excavations have revealed late Saxon graves under the church floor. An exhibition of the restoration work by English Heritage is open in the church (Monday-Friday, Bank Holidays 2.00-4.00pm).

Just E of the church is the brick-built Tyrwhitt Hall, dating from the

15th century, once home to a local branch of the Tyrwhitt family. This contains the timber-framed Great Hall, formerly used on ceremonial occasions. Return along Beck Hill between the two churches, and proceed S along Whitecross Street. This has more interesting town houses from the 18th century and a distinctly historical feel. At least one house has mock neo-classical pillars surrounding its doorway.

On reaching a crossroads turn R for a few yards down Market Lane. On the L side, set slightly back from the road, is the five-storeyed tower of a windmill (known as Tower Mill) minus its sails, and curiously surrounded by other buildings. This is one of three former windmills in the town and would benefit from restoration.

Return to the crossroads and turn R once more into Whitecross Street. A few yards down on the R you will see the painted sign of the Volunteer Inn, with symbolic reference to Egypt and the Napoleonic Wars. Traditionally the volunteers of the Royal Lincolnshire Regiment were known as 'yellow-bellies' after their uniforms, a term which has since gained wide popular usage to describe the stern independence of Lincolnshire folk.

A short distance further down you pass a splendid Queen Anne residence known as Bardney Hall, before reaching the entrance to Baysgarth Park. Here an elegant Georgian house accommodates the local **Baysgarth Museum** (open Thursday-Sunday and Bank Holidays, 10.00-4.00pm, admission free). The displays include pottery fragments from the Anglo-Saxon burial site at Castledyke South and skeletal remains from the former monastery at Barrow on Humber. There is also a military collection and exhibits of European and Oriental porcelain.

Thornton Abbey

Some 5 miles SE of Barton, but well worth a mention in this guide, are the ruins of the 12th century Thornton Abbey, now in the care of English Heritage. Founded by William le Gross in 1139, it became one of the richest monasteries in the region. Its founder was known as the Count of Aumale and Lord of Holderness, a figure of some power and influence who also established several Cistercian houses. Thornton Abbey was created for 'Cannons Regular' of the Augustinian Order, distinguished by their black robes.

Today the remains include the remarkable 14th century crenellated

gatehouse, which has survived almost intact. This is a remarkable edifice: the turrets are of weathered yellow ironstone with narrow windows flanked by brickwork, and the imposing W front has statues of the Virgin Mary, St John the Baptist and other saintly figures. It is possible to explore inside the gatehouse, climbing up the steep and narrow spiral staircase.

The first and second floors have large rooms overlooking the entrance and the grounds. Each has a broad fireplace, seeming to confirm the view that the gatehouse was used by the Abbot for entertaining important guests. Narrow corridors lead off into the N and S wings, with look-out posts in the turrets. Also within the gatehouse is an exhibition of carved stonework fragments from the main Abbey with examples of medieval floor tiles.

The remains of the Abbey buildings are reached by footpath across a meadow to the E. Most of these are visible only at ground level, but it is possible to make out the outline of the Abbey church, cloisters and several annexes. Part of the 14th century Chapter House survives intact, showing its octagonal structure and regular patterns of window tracery.

Life in the Abbey appears to have been fairly uneventful during the four centuries of its life, with many particulars being recorded in the early 16th century chronicle. By this time the Abbey had acquired a considerable wealth, its annual income amounting to nearly £600 just before the Dissolution. The Prior and twenty-seven Cannons were forced to surrender the Abbey in December 1539.

After this, the buildings were converted to a religious college for 'secular' Cannons by order of Henry VIII. Its purpose was to be:

> "for the ministration of the sacraments, the observance
> of good manners, the care of the aged...and for the
> instruction of the young."

This plan, however, lasted only six years until Henry's death in 1545. The monarch is said to have visited briefly with Katherine Howard in 1541, during a tour of Lincolnshire and Yorkshire.

Today Thornton Abbey has a setting which is pleasantly rural, despite the proximity of the Killingholme refineries. In summer the lawns and ruins are often alive with swallows while sheep graze on the intervening meadow. Legend has it that a scholarly monk may sometimes be seen seated at a table in the grounds, in the act of writing with a book, ink-well and feather quill.

Opening Hours

April-September,	Monday-Saturday	9.30-6.30pm,
	Sunday	2.00-6.30pm.

Tel: (0469) 40357.

Access by Car
From Barton, take the A1077 to Barrow on Humber, turn L through the village, then R for 2½ miles down the minor road towards East Halton.

Access by Public Transport
BR station Thornton Abbey on the Barton-Grimsby line.

*   *   *

Barton upon Humber to Barnetby   12 miles

To start the Viking Way, take Waterside Road from Barton railway station, and head for the river. Just round the corner at the **Visitor Centre** is the official start of the route. Nearby are Barton Clay Pits, an extensive area of marshy pools and lakes, part of which is now a Country Park. The Visitor Centre provides information on fishing, watersports and other recreational facilities.

Take the footpath along the embankment heading W. From this point there is a truly magnificent view of the **Humber Bridge**, the arch of the carriageways supported by a criss-cross of seemingly slender cables. Just beyond on the L is the sole surviving tile works, with rows of attractive red pantiles stacked outside.

Further along you will pass a series of lakes and reed beds, presently reaching **Far Ings**, the nature reserve managed by the Lincolnshire and South Humberside Trust for Nature Conservation. There are four public viewing hides and the reserve is home for a variety of water birds and visiting waders.

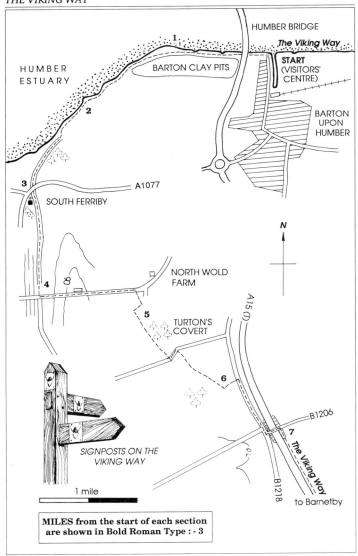

HUMBER BRIDGE

The Viking Way

START
(VISITORS'
CENTRE)

BARTON CLAY PITS

H U M B E R
E S T U A R Y

BARTON
UPON
HUMBER

1

2

3

A1077

SOUTH FERRIBY

N

NORTH WOLD
FARM

4

A15 (T)

5

TURTON'S
COVERT

6

B1206

7

The Viking Way

*SIGNPOSTS ON THE
VIKING WAY*

B1218

to Barnetby

1 mile

**MILES from the start of each section
are shown in Bold Roman Type : · 3**

24

The footpath continues atop the flood embankment, affording views across the vast expanse of the Humber Estuary with its silt-brown mudbanks and muddy water channels. The route then turns briefly inland, before continuing along a chalky track towards South Ferriby. The main course of the Humber sweeps around on both sides of the low-lying Read's Island. This was created in the early 19th century through the natural process of silting up around an abandoned wreck; with the building of flood banks it grew to almost 200 hectares of new farmland. Today the island has one solitary farmhouse. On the ebb tide you may see a procession of coasters heading up towards the Port of Goole, some 15 miles upstream.

One of the earliest forms of navigation on the river was the Humber Keel, a flat-bottomed, square-rigged vessel said to be a descendant of the Viking longboat. Its shallow draught made it suitable for esturine conditions and for use on inland watercourses. Even prehistoric people are known to have built river craft: one of the most significant finds is the North Ferriby boat, dating from the late Bronze Age (around the 8th century BC) and made from wooden planks sewn together with strips of yew.

The Viking Way (waymarked with the Viking helmet symbol) skirts by **South Ferriby**, passing just above the parish church with its small brick-built tower. The village was most likely the site of Roman occupation and, as the name suggests, probably used as a secondary crossing point of the river.

The track rises gradually, passing a chalk quarry with a covered conveyor belt which feeds the product directly down to the cement works in the valley. Continuing S a view unfolds of the broad and flat Ancholme river valley, once marshland but now drained and closely cultivated. In the distance can be seen the towers of Scunthorpe's blast furnaces, etched against the skyline.

On the far side of the valley Ermine Street, the Roman Road, runs with almost geometric precision on its determined course from Lincoln, heading for Winteringham and an ancient crossing point of the Humber. The Romans established a ferry from there in 70 AD which docked at Brough (Roman Petuaria) from where the road continued en route for York.

Just over a mile from South Ferriby the Way turns L along a minor road, climbing the slope of Horkstow Wolds. The hamlet itself

On top of the Wolds near Turton's Covert

shelters at the foot of the slope, and in the late 18th century the site of a Roman villa was discovered nearby, with a fine example of a mosaic pavement. At the top of the ridge the graceful outline of the Humber Bridge reappears, with the cranes of Hull docks far away to the NE. At just over 90 metres (300 feet) this is the highest point on the first stretch of the Way. The surfaced lane descends gently for half a mile, then the route turns R along a double track to head S.

Hereabouts the farming is mainly wheat, barley and beet, with a few sheep. All around are good quality sandy soils with chalky flints, and the fields are mainly open. In spring the Wolds are a pattern of soft greens, and in late summer a vista of golden cornfields splashed with late-flowering poppies. Hares are a common sight, dashing off across the fields. The distant view of the refinery flares at Immingham hardly disturbs the picture of rural peace.

The track continues between fields running SE, past the dense woodland plantation of Turton's Covert. It then skirts briefly E along a surfaced track, before resuming its course alongside a hedgerow with old relict oaks. At about 5½ miles from Barton, the route now

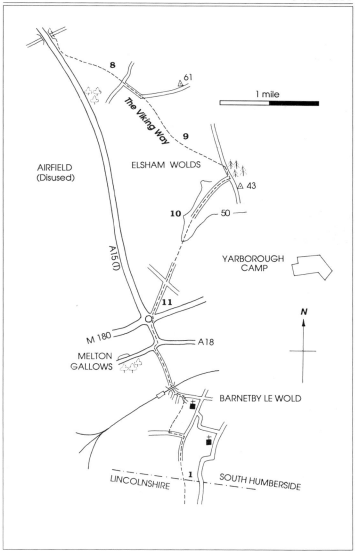

8

△ 61

The Viking Way

1 mile

9

AIRFIELD
(Disused)

ELSHAM WOLDS

△ 43

10

50

A15 (T)

YARBOROUGH
CAMP

11

N

M 180

A18

MELTON
GALLOWS

BARNETBY LE WOLD

LINCOLNSHIRE

1

SOUTH HUMBERSIDE

follows a minor road before crossing the main A15, the dual carriageway which links the M180 with the Humber Bridge.

The route unsatisfactorily follows a hedgeline on the E side of the main road for about a mile before veering SE once again. Although generally well-defined, the footpath along this stretch is sometimes slightly overgrown. The route rejoins a minor road for 400 yards and then continues as a track across farmland, keeping to the edge of the fields.

Here, around Elsham Wolds, the scenery is particularly attractive with the blocks of dark green woodland and shelter belts providing a colour contrast for the crops and brown earth. After a mile the Way emerges beside a small copper beech and turns briefly R down a surfaced lane, with a small coniferous plantation on the L. It then takes a double track SW towards Barnetby. After 1½ miles you cross the roundabout above the Scunthorpe-Grimsby road and the route continues down the minor road into the village.

Just before the Barnetby turning, and a short distance down the old A18 road towards Brigg, is the site of **Melton Gallows**. These were erected in the early 17th century by order of King James I who had resolved to end a conflict between the local families of Ross and Tyrwhitt. Previous hunting expeditions had ended in killings on both sides, so the King decreed that any further deaths would be considered as murder, and the culprits hanged on this spot. Fortunately there is no record of the gallows ever being used, but a simple wooden structure is preserved to this day beside the lay-by.

Barton upon Humber

Accommodation

Humber Bridge Hotel, Ferriby Road.	Tel: (0652) 33991
Westfield Lakes Hotel, Far Ings Road.	Tel: (0652) 32313
George Hotel, George Street.	Tel: (0652) 32433
White Swan Hotel, Fleetgate.	Tel: (0652) 32459
Southgarth (Bed and Breakfast), 2 Caistor Road.	Tel: (0652) 32833

Camping and Caravan Sites

Barton Broads, Chemical Road.	Tel: (0652) 32237
Westfield Lakes, Far Ings Road.	Tel: (0652) 32313

Silver Birches Tourist Park, Waterside Road.   Tel: (0652) 32509

Refreshment
Wheatsheaf Hotel, Holydyke.   Tel: (0652) 33175
The Sloop Inn, Waterside Road.   Tel: (0652) 32581
The Volunteer Arms, Whitecross Street.   Tel: (0652) 32309
The Coach and Horses, High Street.   Tel: (0652) 32161

Access by Car
From the North (M62) and Hull, via the Humber Bridge.
From the South, M180 to Barnetby then the A15 (T).

Access by Public Transport
BR service Grimsby-Barton.   Tel: (0472) 353556
Bus services from Hull (Humber Link) and
Scunthorpe run by Lincolnshire Road
Car Company.   Tel: (0724) 842233

CHAPTER 2
Barnetby to Caistor

Barnetby-le-Wold (See map p27)

This delightfully named village lies in a natural gap of the Wolds, capturing the main lines of communication by road and rail. Three railway lines (from Scunthorpe, Gainsborough and Lincoln) converge from the W, and the line continues E towards Cleethorpes (busy with iron ore for the Scunthorpe steelworks and oil products from Immingham). Railway enthusiasts may also be pleased to see the gantries of semaphore signals still in use at either end of the station.

The Way enters the village down the main street, passing the Railway Inn on the L, with the Station Hotel a short distance further down on the R close to the station yard. Passing under the railway bridge we enter a long street of brick-built houses on Victoria Road, dating from the 19th century. Most of the present village has grown up since the later railway age.

On the corner at the end of Victoria Road is the redbrick structure of **St Barnabas's Church**, built in 1927 as a replacement for the dilapidated medieval church of St Mary's. Inside it has a tall nave with a painted wooden barrel ceiling and there is also a leaden font, said to be a rarity of Norman age. The antiquity of the village is confirmed by the list of parish priests on the W wall, the first being recorded in the 12th century as Walter 'the Priest of Barnethebi'.

From the church turn R along St Barnabas' Road, and 100 yards down on the R you will pass the somewhat neglected former village 'National School' which dates from 1862. Further down the main road swings round to the L, but straight on down Marsh Lane is a small Wesleyan chapel, one of many established in the district in the tradition of John Wesley, the famous Methodist preacher who was born in Epworth.

The main road swings around SE and heads up the slope of the Wolds on the outskirts of the village. High up on a ridge is the original **Church of St Mary**, reached by a short track off to the R. Normally locked, it stands in splendid isolation looking out across the valley. The tower is somewhat truncated and the exterior walls of the nave much repaired; it is not difficult to see why the church was abandoned. In stark contrast are the bright red pantiles of the re-roofed chancel. St Mary's is now maintained by the Redundant Churches Fund.

From here you can return to the centre of the village and rejoin the Way, or take a short cut to the end of Marsh Lane where the route takes a sharp R turn before heading off towards Bigby. Those with transport may wish to visit some of the other attractions in the district. Two miles N of Barnetby is the pleasant dormitory village of Elsham, reached by a minor road from the M180 roundabout.

Just beyond Elsham (off the B1206 Brigg to Ba ɔn road) is the entrance to **Elsham Hall Country Park**, a facility run by Glanford Borough Council. The Park (summer opening 11.30am-5.30pm, adults £1.90, children 90p [1989]) includes a walled garden, bird and butterfly gardens, fishing lakes and a recently planted arboretum containing over eighty tree species. You can also go horse-riding (bookable in advance, Tel: 0652 688698).

Elsham Hall itself dates from the 18th century and is set within attractive grounds. Unfortunately it remains part of a private estate and there is no public access. It is still the home of the Elwes family and was used as a base by Percy Grainger during his travels around Lincolnshire to collect traditional folk songs.

About 2 miles west of Barnetby (on the A18 towards Brigg) is **Wrawby Post Mill**, the only complete example of this type of mill remaining in Lincolnshire. It is situated a quarter of a mile before the centre of Wrawby village, 100 yards down Mill Lane, off the main road to the L. Built in 1760 and restored in 1964, the upper house of the mill is constructed of wooden slats, above a substantial brick base. The six huge sails are fully intact and the whole upper house can be turned in any direction to face the prevailing wind. It is set in a commanding position on a hilltop, with views in each direction. (View the exterior of the mill at any time; the key for the interior is at Mill House opposite. Adults 40p, children 25p [1989]. Tel: 0652 53699.)

A mile beyond Wrawby is the ancient market town of **Brigg**, so-called because of the bridge across the River Ancholme. Early in the

13th century King John granted a charter for an annual fair to be held around the first week of August. This was later immortalised in the traditional folk song, *Brigg Fair*. Most of the present town dates from the 18th and 19th centuries and there are some interesting old inns, although nowadays the narrow streets are quite busy with traffic.

An early Bronze Age boat was discovered near the town in 1866, close to the River Ancholme. Dating from around the 10th century BC (perhaps 200 years before the North Ferriby boat) it was hollowed out in primitive fashion from a solid oak tree, and was certainly one of the earliest vessels of its kind in Britain. Unfortunately it was destroyed in a World War II bombing raid when housed in a museum in Hull.

∗   ∗   ∗

Barnetby to Caistor   8 miles

From Victoria Road the Way diverts down St Mary's Avenue, which is third on the R after the railway bridge. The route proceeds past some houses and heads straight out into the fields. Within half a mile it reaches a surfaced lane where it turns L to the corner of Marsh Lane. It now takes a sharp R turn along a double track, running S towards Bigby at the foot of the Wolds Ridge.

Along the way you cross the county boundary into Lincolnshire, and the route is waymarked across open fields. In summer this section is usually well-defined through growing lines of crops. Later in the year the fields may be ploughed, in which case head straight across following the line of electricity pylons.This part of Lincolnshire was once described in somewhat disparaging terms by John Hillaby as *Plogsland* (literally 'ploughed land'). Fortunately things seem to have changed since the "infernal barbed wire and ploughed up paths" made his life such a misery on the Viking Way *. Half a mile before Bigby the route joins a flinty track, with clear evidence of medieval ridge and furrow ploughing on your L.

Hereabouts the western scarp edge of the Wolds is dotted with a series of springline villages, all possessing in their names the Danish suffix 'by', indicating early occupation under Danelaw. None of the

---

* See *Journey Home* by John Hillaby, Constable (1983)

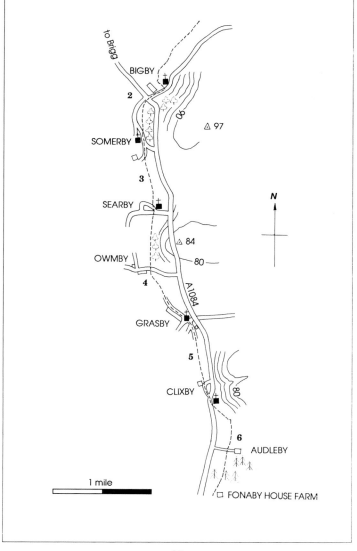

to Brigg

BIGBY

2

SOMERBY

△ 97

3

SEARBY

△ 84

OWMBY

80

4

A1084

GRASBY

5

CLIXBY

80

6

AUDLEBY

1 mile

FONABY HOUSE FARM

N

villages is of any great size and they may once have been little more than collections of farmsteads, linked by trackways, at the foot of the ridge. At **Bigby** the Way joins the village road, and just to the L is the Parish Church of All Saints with its rubble-walled tower. Many churches are now locked during the week, so you may not be able to see the monuments to the local families of Skipwith and Tyrwhitt contained within. The churchyard, however, is a peaceful spot, and often in the background you may hear the contented cooing of doves.

The Way continues S through the village and crosses the A1084 Brigg-Market Rasen road which sweeps directly down from the top of the Wolds. In early season the next field may be ploughed, but later in the year the path runs clearly between the crops. Crossing a stile into the next pasture you approach a limestone monument in the middle of the field. This is over 20 feet high, built in a classical style and topped off with a decorative urn. The monument lacks inscription but is said to commemorate Sir Edward Weston, an 18th century politician who was buried in Somerby churchyard.

Monument near Somerby

Somerby is a tiny hamlet with little remaining besides the farm-house on the site of the former Somerby Manor. The Way passes just above the Parish Church of St Margaret, quaint and diminutive with a short turreted tower and inside the cross-legged effigy of a medie-val knight, possibly a member of the Cumberworth family, one time Lords of the Manor.

The route now follows a minor road and forks R to Grange Farm (at the sign 'No Through Road'). Just before the farm a stile on the L takes you back into the fields as the footpath heads for Searby. To your R are splendid views across the flat agricultural plain of the upper Ancholme Valley. Directly S you can see a distant spur of the Wolds ridge below Caistor.

Just before **Searby** you pass a charming country house on the L, brick-built with rounded window bays. In the village itself St Nicho-las's church is plain from the outside, but this disguises an interesting interior including (on the N wall) a wooden carving of the Last Supper. An inscription records that the wooden loft at the back of the nave was erected in 1732 "at Mrs Roadley's expense." In the N wall a beautiful stained glass window from the 19th century depicts St Nicholas.

Almost directly opposite the church, the route sets off again along a well-defined footpath, reaching a belt of woodland midway up the slope at Owmby Mount and offering more sweeping views away to the SW. Owmby village is passed almost before you realise it, and the track continues a further half a mile to **Grasby**. The fifth of our springline villages, Grasby is slightly larger than the others, the older houses nestling around All Saints church in the centre of the village. **Charles Tennyson Turner**, brother of the more famous Alfred (Lord) Tennyson, was Vicar of Grasby from 1834 until his death in 1879 (see The Tennyson Family History in Chapter 5).

Charles was a poet himself, collaborating with Alfred in *Poems of Two Brothers*, published in 1827 when they both lived at the family home in Somersby. After becoming ordained as a priest his first ap-pointment was that of Curate at Tealby. Later he inherited estates at Caistor and Grasby from his great uncle, in whose honour he adopted the name of Turner. Fortune smiled broadly, for he also moved into his grandfather's former house in Caistor Market Place and for good measure acquired the priesthood at Grasby too.

In 1836 he married Louisa Sellwood, daughter of a well-to-do Horncastle solicitor. At the wedding Alfred Tennyson is said to have become infatuated with Louisa's sister Emily (his future wife), an event which was duly celebrated in verse. All was not well, however, for the newly-married couple: Charles was notorious for his addiction to opium, and there ensued a long separation from his wife which lasted until 1850.

Charles compiled several volumes of verse including a large number of sonnets, the *Collected* version of which was published after his death. His work never received the same popular acclaim as his brother's, but it does stand comparison. The following quotation is taken from *On the Eclipse of the Moon*, written in October 1865:

> "One little noise of life remained - I heard
> The train pause in the distance, then rush by
> Brawling and hushing, like some busy fly
> That murmurs and then settles; nothing stirred
> Beside. The shadow of our travelling earth
> Hung on the silvery moon..."

Alfred Tennyson was a regular visitor to Grasby, especially in the days before his appointment as Poet Laureate. On the W wall of the nave in the parish church there is a commemorative marble plaque to the Tennyson Turner family. This records with gratitude the building of the village school, the new vicarage and the refurbishment of All Saints church. Opposite the church is the village school itself, dating from its last re-building in 1855.

The Way continues through the village, turning R along Clixby Lane, then crossing a stile and heading through cultivated fields for half a mile to Clixby Manor Farm. Hardly anything remains of the original village of **Clixby**, ravaged as it was by the Black Death in the 14th century. Just across the A1084 is the tiny parish church, almost concealed in a bend of the road. Only the chancel remains of what was once a sizeable medieval church, although this fragment has now been carefully restored by the Redundant Churches Fund. Despite its simplicity the church is something of a rough-cut jewel. On the outside the chancel arch can be discerned against the rubble stonework, showing signs of the former nave. The porch was added during a 19th century restoration.

Clixby Church

Inside the stonework is said to date from the early 13th century. The stone-covered altar has a fascinating wooden, painted front depicting scenes from the life of Christ. The painted wooden ceiling appears medieval, but was in fact part of the careful restoration by Hodgson Fowler in 1889. The stone carved font of yellow limestone is an interesting piece with carved saintly figures. It dates from the 15th century, and was introduced from another redundant church at Low Toynton near Horncastle. Of the headstones set in the church floor, the most ancient is a 14th century stone to a priest called Robert Blanchard, with a Latin inscription and the clear outline of a cross and chalice. Despite the proximity of the road, the church has a peaceful atmosphere and a real sense of history held in suspense. A medieval cross adorns the churchyard, with a cruciform top piece.

During the medieval period the plague struck with a suddenness and ferocity which made it one of the worst disasters ever to befall the country. In a short period, around 1348-49, perhaps forty-five per cent of the entire population was wiped out, with whole towns and

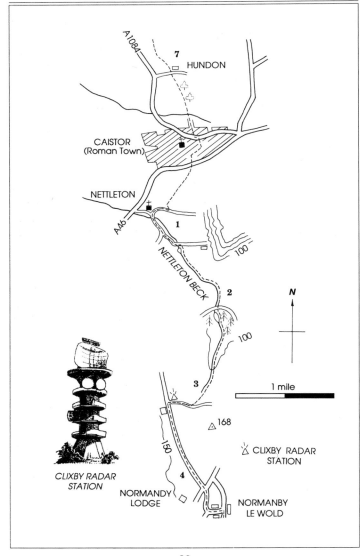

A1084

7

HUNDON

CAISTOR
(Roman Town)

NETTLETON

A46

1

NETTLETON BECK

100

2

100

N

3

1 mile

△ 168

☆ CLIXBY RADAR
STATION

150

*CLIXBY RADAR
STATION*

4

NORMANDY
LODGE

NORMANBY
LE WOLD

38

villages afflicted. The victims developed fever symptoms with black swellings under their arms, and few survived for more than four days. Despite desperate attempts to isolate villages from outside contact, the disease spread more or less unchecked. The population of England was reduced from five to something under three million, and numbers did not fully recover until well into the 15th century.

The fate of Clixby was therefore not uncommon, and plague may have been partly responsible for the abandonment of other villages on the high Wolds (see Chapter 4). One unforeseen result was a labour shortage in the late 14th century which substantially improved the bargaining power of the peasants against the landlords, but that is another story.

Some 30 yards beyond the church, the Way turns L over a stile, crosses first a short meadow and then a long cultivated field. At the far end waymarks indicate the route, which turns briefly E before heading S to the farmstead at Audleby. Here it passes below an elegant country house and resumes a southerly course towards a belt of woodland. Hereabouts the sandy soils are relatively infertile, possibly a contributory factor to the contraction of the original Danelaw settlements.

Beyond the woodland the Way maintains its course, passing a motorcycle scrambling track (usually deserted) on the L. At Fonaby it passes just in front of the farmhouse, then continues across several stiles and a short bridge towards Hundon. The path heads half-way up a short ridge and then crosses the slope S towards the farm buildings (this field is sometimes overgrown).

The Manor farmhouse at **Hundon** is a delightful redbrick affair, no doubt once surrounded by more settlement. Its predecessor was the home of the 14th century Knights *de Hundon* whose effigies lie in the parish church in Caistor. From the farmhouse the route turns briefly R and is then waymarked steeply up a grassy meadow, heading S. Over the rounded hill you follow a line of trees, with the first view of Caistor ahead at the edge of the hills. The route proceeds a further half a mile, descending briefly into a green vale and rising up along a double track into the town.

Accommodation

The Station Hotel, Station Yard, Barnetby.	Tel: (0652) 688238
Arties Mill Lodge, Castlethorpe, Brigg.	Tel: (0652) 52094
The Angel Hotel, Market Place, Brigg.	Tel: (0652) 53118
Lord Nelson Hotel, Market Place, Brigg.	Tel: (0652) 52127

For accommodation in Caistor see Chapter 3.

Refreshment

The Railway Inn, Barnetby.	Tel: (0652) 688284
The Cross Keys Inn, Brigg Road, Grasby.	Tel: (065 262) 247

Access by Car
To Barnetby: M180 or A18 from Scunthorpe, A15 from Lincoln.

Access by Public Transport

BR services to Barnetby from Doncaster, Lincoln and Grimsby.	Tel: (0724) 868784

CHAPTER 3
Caistor to Ludford

Caistor (See map p42)

Caistor is a small town with a long ancestry. Its name derives from the Roman camp which once dominated the site, enclosing an area of some 7 acres just W of the present Market Place. As such it formed a junction between 'High Street', the Romanised ridge-top road from the Humber, and the probable connection to Lincoln via Ermine Street. Most of the present town dates from the 18th and 19th centuries, partly the result of re-building after a disastrous fire in 1681. Nowadays Caistor is quiet and unassuming, but the locals are quite friendly.

The Way enters the town through an alleyway, turning L onto the Main A1084 before branching R into Market Place. This is the town square, the centre of most activities today and little changed since the days of George Tennyson (Alfred Tennyson's grandfather). On the W side of the square is the cream-coloured Georgian mansion once occupied by Mary Turner and reputed to be the place where George Tennyson courted her. A comparison with old prints shows it to be virtually unchanged since the early 19th century. Of more recent origin is the statue of a golden lion which sits atop a black marble base in the centre of the square. This was erected in 1897 for Queen Victoria's Diamond Jubilee. It incorporates the handle of the old parish pump, which has certainly stood here for over a century.

From Market Place, Bank Lane leads W toward the **Parish Church of St Peter and St Paul**, the ironstone tower of which has a small W doorway of Saxon origin, although most of the church dates from the Early English period. Inside in the N aisle are the reclining figures of Sir William and Lady de Hundon. Sir William died in the early 14th century as a veteran of the crusades. His successor, Sir John de Hundon (whose effigy lies nearby) became High Sherrif of Lincolnshire in 1343.

Also on display is the so-called **Gad Whip**, the name of which may be derived from a 'goad', a pointed stick used to drive oxen. This

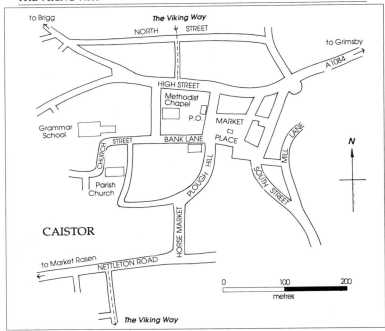

whip was once used for a bizarre custom, the precise origins of which are shrouded in mystery. Every Palm Sunday a man from the neighbouring parish of Raventhorpe would enter the church and crack the whip three times by the porch. To the end of the whip stock he would then tie a small leather purse (containing two shillings), and advance towards the priest giving the lesson. The purse would then be dangled over the priest's head for the rest of the service. In 1846 the practice was suppressed, no doubt as a piece of dangerous superstition.

Caistor is supposed to have some remains of the old Roman walls dating from the 3rd century AD, but these are very elusive. Much easier to find is the old annex of the Grammar School on the N side of the churchyard. This dates from 1631 and has a Latin inscription on its outer wall. The building is still in use as part of the present school. Returning towards Market Place, Chapel Lane leads off to the

L with the huge redbrick Wesleyan chapel, built in a grand neo-classical style, on its R-hand side.

Some 2 miles N of the town on the topmost ridge of the Wolds is **Pelham's Pillar,** a substantial monument to the former Earl of Yarborough who commissioned a large tree-planting scheme in the 1840's. The pillar stands within the private grounds of Brocklesby Park, but at 128 feet high it can be seen from miles around. From Caistor it is approached along the minor road towards Brocklesby (off the A1084 above the N side of the town). The roads hereabouts are good for cycling or driving, with views from the top of the Wolds across the flat lowlands to the W.

✳   ✳   ✳

Caistor to Ludford (See map p38)   12 miles

The Way leaves Market Place in Caistor and proceeds down Plough Hill, then round the corner into Horse Market (a wide street befitting the name). It turns R for a short distance down Nettleton Road and is then signposted L into a small housing estate, emerging on the by-pass road of the A46.

Here the Way goes straight across, then heads down the bank into the next field, notwithstanding the 'Beware of the Bull!' sign on the stile. A footpath leads off R towards the farm, but the Way continues directly ahead, following the field boundary SW in the direction of Nettleton. Stock rearing is common in these fields and the beasts are generally curious but not threatening. Those in doubt could follow the main road round to Nettleton, although this is much less direct.

Nettleton stretches alongside a valley bottom, beside a beck of the same name. On reaching the village road the Way turns L for 400 yards and then takes the L fork along a double track. This leads out of the village and up the valley of Nettleton Beck. Just past a farmhouse on the R the track crosses the stream, then the Way diverts R along a footpath which skirts past a small lake. This valley was once a centre for iron ore extraction and disturbed ground on the opposite bank probably indicates mining activity in the past. The scenery suddenly becomes more remote as fields give way to rough pasture with few signs of habitation. To the E is the resumption of the chalk escarpment, wooded in places.

Further up you reach a young forestry plantation and pass through a 50 yard tunnel. As recently as 1969 iron ores were mined from here; the bricked-up entrances of the adit shafts are visible in the tunnel walls. The path re-emerges into the green vale which is now most distinctively of white chalk. The next mile is a gentle ascent up the valley, veering R across an open meadow close to the ridge-top, then following a double track R towards the road. Turning L beside the radio beacon, the Way follows the road along the summit of the plateau. Around 400 yards E is a trig point in the fields, marking the highest point in Lincolnshire at 168 metres (just over 550 feet).

In the same direction can be seen the slowly revolving tower of Claxby Radar Station. This was completed in 1984 and is used jointly by British Telecom and the Civil Aviation Authority. On clear days glorious views can be had away to the W. After nearly a mile on the road you pass the turning for Thoresway (its name suggestive of Viking origins), and 200 yards further on the Way takes a short cut L across a field to the village of Normanby.

Normanby le Wold, not surprisingly, is the highest village in Lincolnshire, but it consists of little more than a collection of houses and the parish church which is dedicated to **St Peter and St Paul**. Through the village the Way turns R and then L past the churchyard. The church itself is quite pretty, built from the familiar rust-coloured ironstone. At the back of the nave is an octagonal stone front, dating from the 13th-14th centuries and decorated with quatrefoil carving. On the walls are three large but rather faded paintings, one showing the radiant figure of Christ. The most curious piece is the grotesque face carved at the base of an arch in the S aisle. The face, which has a gaping expression and a hand pulling at its mouth, seems to represent toothache! Down the slope of the Wolds in Claxby (the village which gives its name to the local ironstone) the church there has a similar face, no doubt carved by the same artist.

Just opposite Normanby church is a building which looks for all the world like a brick shed, but a second glance reveals the outline of Gothic pointed windows which show that it was indeed a Primitive Methodist chapel. The Way continues S through the fields on a plateau ridge, with excellent views on both sides. Sometimes these

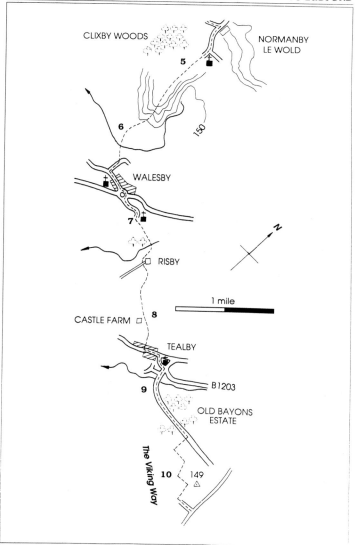

CLIXBY WOODS

NORMANBY
LE WOLD

5

6

150

WALESBY

7

RISBY

1 mile

CASTLE FARM

8

TEALBY

9

B1203

OLD BAYONS
ESTATE

The Viking Way

10 149

N

can extend for 20 miles to the outline of Lincoln Cathedral standing out on the SW horizon. The Way then descends gradually, keeping to the R across a long meadow and passing a sandy bluff which is pock-marked with rabbit burrows Further down, the track levels out on the approach to **Walesby** village.

Reaching the road, the Way turns L into the village and briefly R where the road swings round to climb the hill. Here it diverts L along a wooded track which presently becomes a sunken lane leading up to the old **Parish Church of All Saints**. This is known as the Rambler's Church and commands a magnificent position on the crest of the hill. To the W there are panoramic views across the clay vale towards the distant ridgeline of Lincoln 'cliff'. The church tower (yet another of ironstone) faces W and has withstood the blast of the prevailing winds for more than eight hundred years, although repairs to the fabric are now underway.

In the churchyard is a new beacon stack which commemorates the *Fire over England*, the series of beacons fired in 1588 to warn of the impending arrival of the Spanish Armada. This beacon was re-lit on July 19th, 1988 on the 400th anniversary of the event. The sign itself depicts the Lincolnshire coat of arms (with a Viking longboat, wheat-sheaves and a Roman eagle) and beneath this the motto 'Strive for the good of all'. It is a recent work by a pupil of Caistor Grammer School.

The earliest part of the present church dates from the 12th century, although quoins (or corner stones) at the base of the tower suggest Saxon origins. The chancel was added around 1300, and the clerestory in the 15th century. The church has been badly affected with damp, but in recent years volunteers have made sterling efforts towards internal restoration.

The most intriguing item is the fine stained glass window at the head of the S aisle. This is the **Rambler's Window**, erected in 1950 by members of the Grimsby and District Wayfarers' Association. The scene it shows is almost touching in its innocence: the tall figure of Jesus dominates the centre, flanked by an angelic trio of Sunday ramblers on the L and a pair of cyclists on the R, the very image of piety and good health. In the background is the church, surrounded by golden fields of corn. The window is blessed with a quotation from The Bible.

> "And it came to pass that He went through the
> cornfields on the Sabbath day."
>
> Mark 2 v 23.

Even non-believers will be pleased to learn that rambling has the blessing of the Lord! Since the early 1930's the Lincolnshire Ramblers have held a service in the church on the afternoon of Trinity Sunday (at the end of May), a tradition which continues to this day.

It is tempting to think that the church has always stood in isolation at the top of the hill, but regular banks and ditches in the adjacent field show clear evidence of early medieval settlement. Later the village moved down the hill, and in 1574 the Rector, Thomas Bilcliffe, left 6s 8d (no doubt a reasonable sum then) for the repair of the track up to the church. One of his successors, Robert Burton (1577-1640), became a poet-priest and also penned the religious tract *The Anatomy of Melancholy*, no doubt inspired by the isolation of this remote spot.

The Way passes through the churchyard and heads SE across the next field, past the site of the former village. Crossing a stile the Way is defined across a cultivated field, reaching a woodland after a short distance. Away to the SW there are views across the flat expanse of lowland and the forestry plantations close to Market Rasen.

The path now heads steeply down a grassy bank, which is generally full of rabbits. Looking back from the other side of the vale, the stretch of grassland can be seen topped off with a woody belt. To some this may be reminiscent of the warren in *Watership Down* The Way now passes just below the farmstead of Risby, close to (what appear to be) the ruined garden walls of the old manor, then continues up to the next ridge. Sheep are normally grazed on these slopes, the local variety being large, black-faced and broad-bellied, often with some sort of comical expression on their faces. Here and there are banks and depressions, possibly showing signs of more deserted settlement.

Once over the top of the ridge the path descends beside a woodland, reaching Castle Farm. This building is aptly named, having sturdy rectangular walls and narrow, pointed windows. The Way turns L, heads down to the bottom of a vale and continues across to the next village of Tealby.

Tealby

This is set in the attractive valley of the River Rase, a stream which descends quickly from the Wolds and heads off W towards Market Rasen. From medieval times the village was fairly prosperous, with several watermills dotted along the valley bottom, and in the 19th century it became a centre of the paper-making industry. Half a mile SW is the hamlet of Tealby Thorpe, which has a restored mill dating from the 18th century. Tealby is also notable as the former home of the **Tennyson d'Eyncourt** family. The 'd'Eyncourt' was really an affectation, and requires some explanation.

Charles Tennyson (1784-1861) was the uncle of Alfred (the Poet Laureate) and the younger son of George Tennyson, a prosperous solicitor of Market Rasen. Charles entered the legal profession himself and later became a Liberal MP, a position which he held for thirty-five years. His father was intent on claiming descent from the Baronial family of d'Eyncourt, with a tenuous link through his grandmother's parents. To this end he acquired Bayon's Manor, a former d'Eyncourt property in Tealby. The estate (just S of Tealby village) comprised only a modest Regency house and the small ruins of a medieval castle. Using his son's influence in Parliament, George submitted a petition for the adoption of the d'Eyncourt name, and plans were made for the re-creation of the castle in the image of his supposed forebears.

However, after George's death in 1835 the family inheritance was divided up, the lion's share (including Bayon's Manor) going to Charles, with other property and monies split between the Somersby Tennysons. In the same year Charles received the license to adopt the name and insignia of d'Eyncourt, and before long building work began in earnest.

Over the course of the next few years the small ruins were transformed into a mock medieval castle of grandiose proportions complete with a tower, moat, drawbridge, portcullis and ruined keep. Architectural styles were deliberately varied in order to create the impression of continuous occupation over the centuries. The interior was sumptuously decorated with tapestries and *objets d'art*, and a herd of deer were kept in the grounds. This might be considered the height of pretension.

In Parliament Charles Tennyson was lambasted as 'a man of the

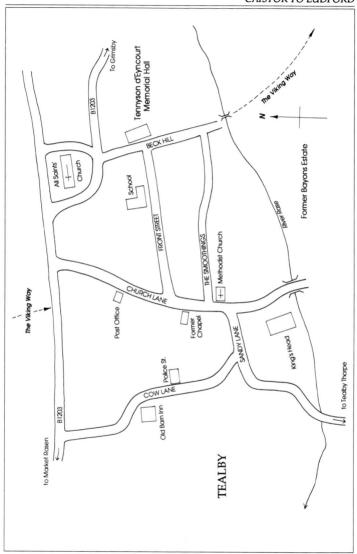

people', a deliberately sarcastic claim which scarcely fitted his opulent lifestyle. He married Frances Hutton and, of their seven children, their son Edwin Clayton rose to the rank of Admiral. Charles's favourite and youngest son, Eustace, died of yellow fever whilst serving with the 46th Regiment in Barbados, an event which prompted his father to compose a lengthy elegiac poem published in 1851. There was little love lost between Charles and his nephew Alfred, although this did not prevent Alfred from seeking the d'Eyncourt title on his uncle's death.

The **Parish Church of All Saints** was restored during the 19th century at the expense of the Tennyson d'Eyncourts and contains a number of memorial tablets. Charles and his wife Frances are buried in the family vault beside the N wall of the chancel. The inscriptions wax lyrical on their character and achievements. Charles we are told was:

> "Courteous and hospitable to his neighbours,
> To the Poor, always considerate and kind."

He is also credited with the building of the village school. Their sons and daughters are remembered with similar eulogies, as is the

The King's Head - an ancient Inn at Tealby

elder George Tennyson. The E window of the chancel displays the claimed heraldry of the d'Eyncourts, with coats of arms illustrated in stained glass.

The remainder of the village has many period cottages in a variety of styles. Opposite the S side of the church on Beck Hill is the Tennyson d'Eyncourt Memorial Hall, attractively built for the use of the parish. Turning off to the R is Front Street, which runs W passing a former Methodist chapel on the R (now a private house) and an existing chapel of the same denomination further down on the L. Just beyond this is the **King's Head**, a traditional pub dating from 1397. This has a splendid thatched roof and whitewashed walls, a reminder of how some of the houses may have looked a hundred years ago. The return to Beck Hill can be made along the curiously named side street known as The Smootings.

Tealby to Ludford (See map p45)
From the parish church the Way runs down Beck Hill, reaching the river at a delightful ford and crossing by means of the footbridge. The track directly ahead leads into the old Bayon's Manor Estate. It is a pity that little remains of the former castle, a view shared by some of the locals who can remember it in a semi-ruined state from twenty years ago. It was described in some detail in Pevsner's 1964 edition of *The Buildings of England*, its assortment of architectural styles being summed up as "the mingling of scholarship and amateurism." After several years of neglect it was finally raised to the ground in 1970. The Way passes through the old parkland, with the foundations of the Manor in amongst the woodland to the L of the track. Nowadays the ground is often thick with pheasants, an over-population caused by artificial breeding.

The Way follows the track over the brow of a hill, but turns R before the top of the next ridge. From here it zig-zags along footpaths for the next mile, crossing the hill and in due course reaching the ridge-top road of High Street. It turns R along the road for 100 yards before taking a footpath L into the adjacent field (at the road junction a quarter of a mile further on are the Boucherette Tea Rooms). The path runs E for nearly half a mile, then heads S into the village of Ludford.

Market Rasen

The small size of the town (population 3,500) belies its significance as a market centre, for it serves a vast rural area of the Lincolnshire Clay Vale and the Central Wolds. Most of the town is pleasantly historic, with some interesting 19th century and Georgian buildings. It straddles the main A631 road from Gainsborough which continues W across the Wolds towards Louth.

The charter giving the right to hold markets in the town was isued in 1215 and it is still exercised to this day with the Tuesday market. Close to the railway station on Chapel Street is the remarkable facade of the Centenary Methodist Church, featuring Ionic columns in a neo-classical style.

One mile E of the Market Rasen is the racecourse, used regularly for steeplechasing in the National Hunt series. Much of the land at the foot of the Wolds has wind-blown sands from the former Triassic deserts, and in consequence there are extensive woodland plantations, owned by the Forestry Commission. There are two campsites here within fairly easy reach of the Viking Way.

Accommodation

Red Roofs Guest House, Horncastle Road, Caistor.	Tel: (0472) 851284
Windrush, 99 Brigg Road, Caistor.	Tel: (0472) 851278
Boucherette Farm, North Willingham. (B&B and Tea Rooms)	Tel: (067 383) 538
Gordon Arms Hotel, Queen Street, Market Rasen.	Tel: (0673) 842364
The White Swan Hotel, Queen Street, Market Rasen.	Tel: (0673) 843356

Refreshment

The Red Lion, Market Place, Caistor.	Tel: (0472) 851205
The White Hart Hotel, 21 South Street, Caistor.	Tel: (0472) 851734
The King's Head, Sandy Lane, Tealby.	Tel: (067 383) 347
Jossals Cafe, King Street, Market Rasen.	

Caravan and Camping Sites

Red Roofs, Horncastle Road, Caistor.	Tel: (0472) 851284
Nettleton Park, Nettleton, nr Caistor.	Tel: (0472) 851501
Walesby Woodlands, Walesby Grange, Market Rasen.	Tel: (0673) 843285
Market Rasen Racecourse, Legsby Road.	Tel: (0673) 843434

Access by Car
To Caistor: A46 from Market Rasen, A1084 from Brigg.
To Market Rasen: A46 from Lincoln, A631 from Louth.

Access by Public Transport

Bus service Lincoln-Market Rasen, Lincoln City Transport.	Tel: (0522) 3444
Bus service Lincoln-Caistor, Lincolnshire Road Car Co.	Tel: (0522) 532424
BR services from Lincoln and Barnetby to Market Rasen.	Tel: (0522) 39502

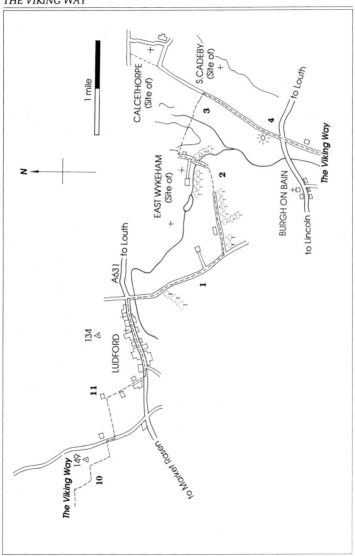

CHAPTER 4

Ludford to Scamblesby

Ludford to Scamblesby   11miles
Reaching the A631 (Market Rasen to Louth road) the Way turns L
through **Ludford**, with the village extending like a ribbon along the
main road. Its full name is Ludford Magna, and the stretch of road is
Magna Mile. On the L you pass a garden centre cafetería, and further
along on the R an official Viking Way car park down Playing Field
Lane. There are two inns (The Black Horse and The White Hart), and
between these on the L is a small marble memorial stone to the airmen
of RAF 101 Squadron, stationed here during World War II.

Just beyond the village the Way turns R along the road to Burgh on
Bain. For just over a mile it follows this broad lane with wide verges,
then turns L by a belt of woodland. The route passes Girsby Top Farm
and heads into the valley of the infant River Bain. In the valley itself
is a wooded plantation, just beyond which on the L are the open
meadows of Wykeham Hall.

The Landscape now has the appearance of parkland, but long
ridges and banks on the hillside are clear signs of the former medieval
village of **East Wykeham**. An unfenced track leads W to the Hall,
close to which are the foundations of the old village church. This area
has a positive sprinkling of lost or deserted villages: half a mile to the
W is the site of West Wykeham, whilst $1^1/_2$ miles E are the distinct
remains of Calcethorpe. Yet another village, South Cadeby, was sited
1 mile S of there, close to a tributary of the River Bain.

The subject of lost medieval villages has now become a fascinating
aspect of archaeological research and over 7,000 sites have been
recorded in England and Wales. There are many possible causes put
forward for their decline including the Black Death, climatic change
and the effects of the Hundred Years' War. The principle reason,
however, was almost certainly land enclosures made mainly in the
late 15th and early 16th centuries, prompted by new demands for
British wool. Thus the old medieval pattern of strip cultivation in

open fields was swept away and many peasant families were forced off the land to seek employment in the towns.

Enclosures were regarded as a social evil and likened to the work of the devil, a view reflected with bitter irony in this popular 16th century verse:

> "Commons to close and keep,
> Poor folk for bread do cry and weep,
> Towns pulled down to pasture sheep,
> This is the new guise.
>
> Envy waxeth wondrous strong,
> The rich doeth the poor wrong,
> God of his mercy suffereth long,
> The devil his work to work."

Anon.

In a classic work published in 1954 *, Maurice Beresford examined much of the documentary evidence of village decline, especially for the late medieval period of the 14th-16th centuries. In spite of more recent excavation and survey work, this book remains one of the principal sources of reference and has never been bettered. Beresford estimated a figure of thirty-four lost villages in this part of Lincolnshire, with a concentration of sites in the higher parts of the Wolds.

East and West Wykeham appear to have been in decline soon after the Black Death, and both villages had less than ten families by 1428. Accordingly the Bishop of Lincoln declared a union with the larger village of Ludford Magna, and no new priests were instituted. Calcethorpe lost its parish church before 1450 and by 1563 was down to just four families. Meanwhile Calceby (9 miles S of Louth) still had eighteen families in 1563, but eventually all settlement was abandoned, leaving just the ruins of the village church.

Plague may have started the process of decline (the worst outbreaks of disease took place in the mid 14th century, 1348-1369) but depopulation continued for at least the next 200 years. The soils were perhaps marginal for cultivation, but it seems likely that peasant farming was progressively ousted by sheep pastures. With further 'Parliamentary' enclosures in the 18th century the transformation

---

* M W Beresford, *The Lost Villages of England*, Lutterworth (1954).

was complete.

During his visit in 1830 Cobbett reported seeing great flocks of sheep up to 1,000 strong. A pattern of open pastures with furze is also apparent from some of Tennyson's poetic description of the higher Wolds. Arable farming was by no means redundant in the 19th century, but it is only in comparatively recent years that the higher Wolds ridges have returned to the plough. Of the medieval villages little remains above ground today, and a certain degree of imagination is required to picture the old pattern of streets and houses.

Leaving the site of East Wykeham, the Way is signposted R just beyond a house and heads off along a field boundary, going into a dip and rising up to the next ridge. At the ridge-top track a diversion can be made L for half a mile towards **Calcethorpe Manor Farm**.

A footpath continues NE for a short distance, with the ridges and hollows of the former village enclosed within a meadow on the R. This was a sizeable settlement, approximately 400 metres square, and ground studies have revealed a clear pattern of streets and alleyways. The best time to visit the site is in early summer - before the long grass obscures some of its features.

Returning along the same track, the Way continues SW passing Grim's Mound, a Bronze Age round barrow used as a burial chamber. Hereabouts the Wolds are dissected by the small tributaries of the Bain, with the highest ridge of chalk in the E. Away to the SW on a secondary ridge is the Belmont TV mast, which at 1,265 feet is still one of the tallest in Europe. It was built in the 1960's and nowadays transmits programmes for Yorkshire Television.

The Way now crosses the A157 (Louth to Lincoln road) and makes a gentle descent along the lane towards Biscathorpe. On the R is a partly disused sand quarry. **Biscathorpe** is yet another lost village site and, as the Way turns L to follow the clear stream of the Bain, there are extensive ridge and hollow remains on the opposite bank. Today there is no village at all, just a house and the tiny estate church of St Helen's, built in 1844. The church, which is almost hidden in yew trees, is oddly decorated with miniature neo-Gothic spires.

The Way continues R past the church, over a meadow and then across the stream at the footbridge. This pleasant green vale is as quiet and deserted as anywhere on the route. The footpath runs beside a fishing lake and then follows the reed-grown course of the

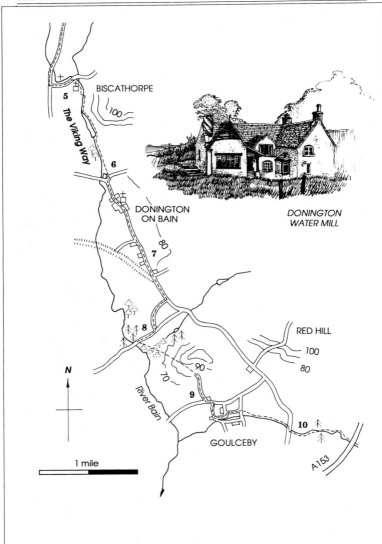

BISCATHORPE

The Viking Way

DONINGTON
ON BAIN

DONINGTON
WATER MILL

RED HILL

N

River Bain

GOULCEBY

A153

1 mile

5
6
7
8
9
10

Bain. Before long you emerge beside Donington Water-mill, an attractive building with whitewashed walls and a red pantiled roof. It has long ceased to be used as a mill, but legend says that it is haunted by the ghost of a murdered woman.

Donington on Bain is a reasonably sized village, with two shops and a pub. Its chunky little church is dedicated to St Andrew and survives as a simple nave and tower, dating from the Early English period of the 12th-13th centuries. The exterior shows clear signs of a former N aisle which may have been demolished in the 18th century. It is thought that the earliest church, and possibly the original village, were sited further E at the foot of the Wolds ridge in a field known as Kirkfloor. Inside the present building is a barrel-shaped stone font, dating from the late Saxon or early Norman period.

The church was also home to a long deceased custom. Until the 18th century it was traditional to throw hassocks at the bridal party as they entered the church. The practice ended abruptly in 1780 when the Rector himself was hit by a flying hassock! The Way runs through the village and continues S along the road towards Scamblesby. In just under a mile you reach the old station yard of the Lincoln-Louth railway, closed to passengers in 1951. Away to the SE Stenigot House is visible at the foot of the chalk escarpment, set in wooded country. High on the ridge is Stenigot Beacon, a radio mast used by the RAF.

Around 400 yards beyond the old station the Way turns R along the lane signposted to Market Stainton. This passes through an attractive belt of coniferous forest and runs down into the valley. Just before a second wood the Way is signposted L along a field's edge. The route then passes through a belt of poplars before crossing a stream and heading up a damp meadow on Colley Hill. At the top of the hill it joins a double track which winds scenically around towards Goulceby. At the road the Way turns L (passing a small wayside chapel) and then R into the village. **Goulceby** is a scattered settlement with many new houses. The Way turns L just before the village stream, but 100 yards further on is The Three Horse Shoes (which has a small campsite).

A mile NE of Goulceby is the Nature Reserve of **Red Hill**, a small grassland site managed by the Lincolnshire and South Humberside Trust. This is located on the crest of the chalk ridge and is reached along the minor road towards Raithby. Its name is derived from an unusual outcrop of Red Chalk, which is clearly visible as you approach uphill from the SW. The site was originally a chalk pit, but now provides one of the few remaining fragments of chalk grassland in the Wolds.

The flowering plants here include yellow wort, pyramidal orchid and autumn gentian. The author has also witnessed a grass snake crossing the road! The vantage point provides sweeping views across the valley of the Bain and further down the Wolds ridge. Oddly enough Red Hill Quarry is also the site of an annual Good Friday service, attended by parishoners from the nearby hamlet of Asterby who carry with them three symbolic wooden crosses.

Back in Goulceby the Way proceeds to the E side of the village then continues along a footpath, passing through fields beside the stream (Red Hill is visible briefly to the NE). After half a mile you reach a minor road and the route follows the S bank of the stream, going through a short belt of woodland.

Before long the Way rejoins the N bank and emerges on the main A153 (Horncastle-Louth) road. Nearby, the fertile alluvial soils are sometimes used for the cultivation of tulips. Turn R along the main road for 400 yards and then L into the village of **Scamblesby**. There is Bed and Breakfast accommodation to be had in the village, with the alternative of Woody's Top Youth Hostel, which lies 3 miles SE on a high ridge of the Wolds (open every day in summer but booking is advisable).

Louth

This is a fine old market town at the E edge of the Wolds, some 6½ miles from Burgh on Bain on the A157. As an original Scandinavian settlement its name may be derived from a Norse pronunciation of Lud (as 'Luth'), after the river on which the town stands. In medieval times Edward VI provided the town's charter, and Henry II granted a concession for two annual fairs, which produced a flourishing trade in wool and wine.

The most striking monument to late medieval prosperity is the elegant tower and steeple of **St James' Church**, built between 1501-15. At 295 feet this is some 20 feet *higher* than the central tower of Lincoln Cathedral, and is perhaps the tallest spire of any English parish church. Also worthy of mention is the Grammar School, which dates back to 1276. Its more famous pupils have included the explorer Sir John Franklin (who later died in the search for the North-West Passage), and the Tennyson brothers Alfred and Charles. The original school (rebuilt in 1869) stands on Schoolhouse Lane at the E end of the town.

Louth is remembered for its part in the Lincolnshire Rising of 1536. In this, the so-called Pilgrimage of Grace, religious discontent was combined with popular resentment of land enclosures, and the rebellion soon commanded the support of 40,000 men. In Louth the revolt was led by Nicholas Melton, a shoemaker who took the name of Captain Cobbler. It was also given blessing by the local vicar, Thomas Kendall. The rebels joined forces with others from Caistor and Horncastle and advanced towards Lincoln.

There they submitted a petition to the King, listing their grievances. Henry VIII's reaction was one of outrage and shock. The rebels were condemned as "the rude commons of one of the most brute and beastly shires of the realm," and a loyal army was dispatched to deal with them. The rising then collapsed and severe retribution was taken against some of its leaders, including the unfortunate Thomas Kendall.

Accommodation

The White Hart, Ludford.	Tel: (050 781) 664
Southwold, Donington on Bain.	Tel: (050 784) 394
Coppers End, Scamblesby.	Tel: (050 784) 222
The Old Vicarage, Scamblesby.	Tel: (050 784) 790
Woody's Top Youth Hostel, Ruckland.	Tel: (0205) 68651 for bookings.

Refreshment

The Black Horse, Ludford.	Tel: (050 781) 645
The Black Horse, Donington on Bain.	Tel: (050 784) 640
The Three Horse Shoes, Goulceby.	Tel: (050 784) 610
The Marshall Arms, Scamblesby.	Tel: (050 784) 282

Camping/Caravan Sites

The Three Horse Shoes, Goulceby.	Tel: (050 784) 610

Access by Car
To Ludford: A631 from Market Rasen or Louth.

Access by Public Transport
Bus service Lincoln-Ludford-Louth,
Lincoln City Transport.(Only 1 bus per day.) Tel: (0522) 53444

Bus service Lincoln-Burgh on Bain-Louth,
Lincolnshire Road Car Co.   Tel: (0522) 532424

CHAPTER 5

Scamblesby to Horncastle

Scamblesby to Horncastle   8 miles

The village of Scamblesby is quiet and low lying, being by-passed by the main road. The Way turns S and follows the village road for half a mile, with the houses somewhat strewn out. The predominant landscape feature remains the chalk escarpment to the E which rises abruptly from the valley floor. A road turns L in the village, leading directly up the escarpment towards Woody's Top Youth Hostel high up on the plateau some 3 miles distant. Nowadays this is big farming country with large open fields and over-sized tractors to suit. In late summer the plateau tops are a vast expanse of golden cornfields, though the soils themselves are thin and hardly suited to cereals.

On his travels in 1830 William Cobbett passed through here, remarking of Scamblesby that:

"The vale in which it lies is very fine land... This is very fine corn country: chalk at the bottom, stony near the surface, here and there a chalk pit in the hills, the shape of the land somewhat like that of the broadest valleys in Wiltshire."

The description almost fits the landscape of today, although suffice to say that the land is more closely cultivated and sheep farming on the higher slopes has receded under the plough. The buildings, however, are quite different. In Cobbett's time the houses were "white and thatched, as they are in all chalk countries."

The Way continues S out of the village along a double track, keeping R as it climbs up an open field, passing close to woodland on the right. It reaches a ridge top just W of Park Hill, then remains well-defined as it descends into a gentle vale towards Belchford.

The land certainly is very fine, the overlying glacial deposits producing good quality loam soils, rarely out of cultivation. Descending towards Belchford a short post beside the track is the only sign of the underground North Sea gas pipeline: an admirable piece of environmental planning. Also invisible is the speculated line of the Roman road which ran SE (almost through Belchford itself) joining Lincoln

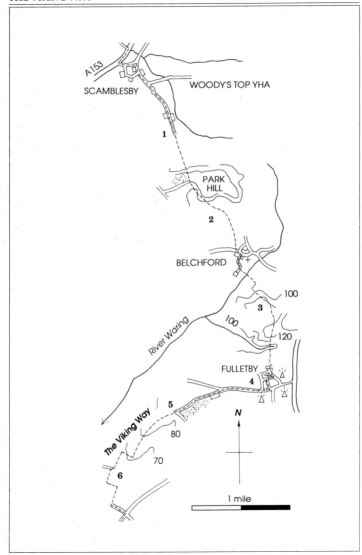

A153
SCAMBLESBY
WOODY'S TOP YHA
1
PARK
HILL
2
BELCHFORD
100
3
100
120
River Waring
FULLETBY
4
The Viking Way
5
80
70
6
N
1 mile

Late evening at Biscathorpe, Lincolnshire Wolds
The view towards Belchford, Lincolnshire Wolds

The Viking Way near Woodhall Spa

Isaac Newton's birthplace at Woolsthorpe by Colsterworth

with Burgh le Marsh.

The village of **Belchford** clusters around the post office and the Blue Bell Inn, which is presently reached along the Way. Just around the corner the parish church (another dedicated to St Peter and St Paul) is a very basic, chapel-like structure built from the local green-sand. Following the Lincolnshire Rising in 1536 serious punishment was meted out to some of its leaders: the Rector of Belchford was hung, drawn and quartered after refusing to recognise Henry VIII as head of the English Church.

From the post office the Way turns R down Dams Lane, then L over a stile just before a farmhouse. Crossing the tiny stream of the River Waring, the path ascends a short hill, swinging R and then L before continuing up an easy ridge in the direction of Fulletby. From here there are views back to the shallow vale, with rolling hills beyond.

At the top of the ridge the Way is signposted R along a field edge, descending another vale before rising through lush pastures to **Fulletby**. The Way turns R and passes the Parish Church of St Andrew's, another simple structure of dark-coloured greensand, most of it dating from the early Victorian era. Inside, the carved font and reredos (altar screen) are works by Richard Winn, the former village blacksmith. His brother Henry was a most noted local figure, being a schoolmaster, poet and Parish Clerk for no less than seventy-six years. He died in 1914 at the age of 98 and a memorial plaque is dedicated to him on the N wall of the nave.

Fulletby stands on a high ridge (at about 450 feet), a prime spot for the radio masts on the edge of the village. There are no shops, only a petrol station on the topmost road. Those wishing to camp should perhaps take a diversion here to the nearest site, The Cross Keys Inn at Salmonby (half a mile N of Salmonby on the outskirts of Tetford). Tennyson's birthplace is a further 1½ miles SW along minor roads in the village of Somersby.

The Way now turns W and descends gently for half a mile down a minor road, then takes the L fork signposted to Grange Farm. Past the farm it continues as a double track, passing a mature belt of wood-land which abounds with breeding pheasant. It then follows a green path along the backbone of a broad ridge, looking directly ahead into the vast expanse of the Horncastle Vale. It zig-zags down an easy gradient towards the town, with the tower of West Ashby church

Tennyson's birthplace at Somersby

visible away to the R. Presently you cross a short bridge ov.
(erected by the Horncastle group of the Rambler's Associa   n
1985) and, although the path may be slightly overgrown, you sh uld
skirt L along the edge of a field. The Way then turns S once again into
an open pasture before turning L towards the minor road which is
followed for the last mile into Horncastle.

Somersby and the Tennyson Country

Somersby and Bag Enderby lie at the very heart of Tennyson Country
in the upper valley of the River Lymn. Those walking the Way can
take a diversion at Fulletby, but Somersby is 3¹/₂ miles away along
minor roads, so your own transport would be a definite advantage.
Those driving from Horncastle should take the A158 Skegness road
for 1¹/₂ miles, turning L at High Toynton, then follow the minor road
to Salmonby, taking the R fork just after the village. Somersby is then
a further mile down the valley.

  Today the village is little more than a tiny hamlet, set in pleasant
wooded country suggestive of parkland. Approaching from Salmonby, you first pass the Old Rectory on the R. This, Tennyson's
original home, is now privately owned and known as Somersby

House. It is attractively built of cream-painted brickwork and set behind substantial hedgerows. A few yards further down is the Parish Church of St Margaret's, small and built of weathered green-sand. The village was never large, but rural depopulation has reduced the number of inhabitants from an estimated three hundred in the early 19th century, to less than seventy today.

The interior of the church has several interesting items of Tennyson memorabilia, and other decorative works. At the front of the nave stands a bronze bust of the bard himself, a bearded figure in middle age. This is a replica of Woolner's original sculpture which is kept at Trinity College, Cambridge. On the N wall of the chancel is a plaque commemorating Tennyson's father, George Clayton, who served as Parish Priest from 1806-1830. On the opposite wall, and from a rather earlier age, there is an intricate brass etching showing the kneeling figure of George Littlebury, a local worthy and 'Seventh Son' who died in 1612.

Perhaps the most striking item is the reredos hung on the N wall at the back of the nave. This is a copy of the remarkable painting by Hubert van Eyck, commissioned for the parish church in Ghent in the early 15th century, and thought to have been inspired by the Book of Revelation. The painting is in four sections and shows over three hundred figures (including chivalrous knights, high churchmen and priests) all assembled in witness to the Lamb of God, a curious looking beast placed on top of the sacrificial altar.

Also within the nave there are further Tennyson artifacts displayed in a glass case. These include a feather quill used for his compositions and two of his famous clay pipes. In the churchyard just outside the porch is a restored medieval cross, with a diamond-shaped head piece and the worn figure of a bishop. Just opposite the church (and next door to the Old Rectory) is an interesting redbrick house known as the Grange, complete with mock embattlements. This is early 18th century in origin and attributed in style to Thomas Vanburgh.

The Tennyson Family

The Tennyson connection with Somersby began early in the 19th century when George Clayton (Alfred Tennyson's father) acquired the priesthood of the parish. He was also Rector of Benniworth and of the Parish of Bag Enderby, so the family lived on a comfortable income and were able to afford a carriage and servants. George married Elizabeth Fytch and they had twelve children, with Charles (later the Vicar of Grasby) being born in 1808 and Alfred the following year.

From an early age the children were encouraged to write verse by their mother and father. Alfred was something of a precocious young talent. Having learned to recite Horace's Odes from his father, he was then inspired by Pope and began to write verse from the age of eight. Four years later he was composing a six thousand line epic poem in the style of Sir Walter Scott, and soon acquired the habit of a prodigious output. In 1816 he was sent with his brother Charles to the grammar school in Louth.

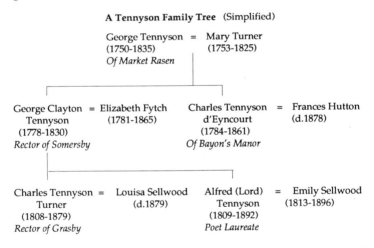

A Tennyson Family Tree (Simplified)

George Tennyson = Mary Turner
(1750-1835)   (1753-1825)
Of Market Rasen

George Clayton = Elizabeth Fytch   Charles Tennyson = Frances Hutton
Tennyson   (1781-1865)   d'Eyncourt   (d.1878)
(1778-1830)   (1784-1861)
Rector of Somersby   *Of Bayon's Manor*

Charles Tennyson = Louisa Sellwood   Alfred (Lord) = Emily Sellwood
Turner   (d.1879)   Tennyson   (1813-1896)
(1808-1879)   (1809-1892)
Rector of Grasby   *Poet Laureate*

In keeping with the nature of the times, George Clayton *purchased* the degree of Doctor of Civil Law, thereafter becoming a Magistrate in Spilsby. Life in Somersby, however, was no paradise of culture and learning: Tennyson's father was prone to epilepsy and ill-health and he often resorted to drink and opium. His temper was notorious, with violent outbursts even against his own family. In 1828 he was finally persuaded to give up his parish duties to seek a health cure in

Switzerland. Such was his fate that he died two years later, soon after his return to Somersby.

In spite of this, Alfred's reputation blossomed and at Cambridge he was awarded the Chancellor's Medal for the poem *Timbuctoo*. His first volume, *Poems of Two Brothers,* was written in collaboration with Charles and published in Louth in 1827. Around this time Alfred's Cambridge friend, Arthur Hallam, was a regular visitor to Somersby for he sought the hand of Alfred's younger sister, Emily. However, Arthur died suddenly on holiday in Venice, an event which had a profound impact on the young Tennyson. He began to compose the lengthy elegiac poem *In Memorium,* which was finally published to popular acclaim in 1850. Later he christened his first son Hallam.

In *In Memorium* Tennyson suffused the imagery of autumn with that of his personal sadness, against a backdrop which seems to evoke the Lincolnshire Wolds:

> "Calm is the morn without a sound,
> Calm as to suit a calmer grief,
> And only thro' the faded leaf,
> The chestnut pattering to the ground.
>
> Calm and deep peace on this high wold,
> And on these dews that drench the furze,
> And all the silvery gossamers,
> That twinkle into green and gold."

Queen Victoria is said to have gained personal solace from reading this poem after the death of Prince Albert.

On the death of his grandfather in 1835 Alfred inherited a manor and small estate at Grasby. However, the properties were later sold and the money invested in a loss-making business venture, which left him almost bankrupt. Despite his established reputation it was also difficult for him to achieve a reliable income from his published works.

During this time Tennyson travelled a great deal and lived in various places in southern England. He also received treatment for his nervous depression, a condition not thought to be improved by his prodigious appetite for pipe smoking. Eventually, with Gladstone's blessing, he accepted a Civil List pension of £200 per year, but it was not until his appointment as Poet Laureate in 1850 that fame and fortune were assured.

In this same year Alfred finally married his long-time sweetheart, Emily Sellwood. They later moved to the Isle of Wight, where they received visits from the Queen and a host of literary figures. With a substantial income they were then able to build a grandiose Gothic mansion at Aldworth in Sussex, which became their first residence. With a supposed dislike of privilege, Tennyson three times turned down a Baronetcy (presumably in the hope of a Peerage, which finally arrived in 1884).

Tennyson's pre-occupation with mythical themes is well known. A fascination with Arthurian legend led to *The Lady of Shalott* and his own version of *Morte d'Arthur* after the epic by Malory. His fondness for the Lincolnshire landscape is also a recurring theme. A passage from *Ode to Memory* recalls a vision of Somersby and the brook which runs below the rectory:

> "Come from the woods that belt the gray hill-side,
> The seven elms, the poplars four,
> That stand beside my father's door,
> And chiefly from the brook that loves,
> To purl o'er matted cress and ribbed sand..."

The poem continues:

> "Pour round mine ears the livelong bleat,
> Of the thick-fleecèd sheep from wattled folds,
> Upon the ridgèd Wolds..."

Tennyson died in 1891 at the age of eighty-two and was laid to rest in Westminster Abbey.

Bag Enderby

Just half a mile SE of Somersby is the equally tiny parish of Bag Enderby, whose present population is less than twenty. Here the greensand stone of the parish church has suffered severe weathering, but as at Somersby there are several interesting items worth seeing. The present church (dedicated to St Margaret) was built with monies left by Albinus de Enderby, a former squire who died in 1407.

There is an iron boss (once part of a shield) fixed to the heavy inner door in the church porch. This is reputed to date back as far as Anglo-

Saxon times, but if so it has withstood the test of time remarkably well! Inside the church there is a carved limestone font which displays heraldic shields, eagles, deer and the figures of the prieta (Christ held in his mother's arms after the crucifixion).

Parts of the original 15th century chancel screen have survived and the church windows show fragments of medieval glass from Crowland Abbey. On the N wall of the chancel is a fine relief carving dedicated to the Gedney family of the late 16th century. It shows the kneeling figures of Andrew Gedney and his wife, Dorothy, flanked by their sons and daughters. All are wearing ruffs in the distinctive Tudor style, the women with long flowing dresses and the men with breeches. Rather less endearing is the small skull which is carved just below the figures.

Nowadays the Tennyson Society still conducts regular 'pilgrimages' to Somersby and Bag Enderby. The biannual commemorative service, held in one of the two churches, is normally very well attended.

Horncastle (see map p 72)

This is a sizeable market town with a history dating back to the arrival of the Roman Ninth Legion in 61 AD. As *Banovallum* it became a garrison town at a crossing point of the River Bain, close to the confluence with its small tributary, the Waring. There were connections by road to Lincoln and along the Romanised 'High Street' to the Humber. The town walls originally enclosed an area of 7 acres around the present day Market Place.

In the 13th century Horncastle received a market charter from Henry III, and trade thereafter became the town's principal function There was a traditional *horse fair* held each August, when gypsies would converge on the town from far and wide, settling their deals with a slap of the hand. This was described in George Borrow's novel *Romany Rye*, which uses Horncastle as its setting. Visitors to the town also included William Cobbett, who passed through in 1830 describing it as:

> "a purely agricultural town, well built and not mean in
> any part of it...a great rendezvous for horses and cattle, and
> sheep dealers."

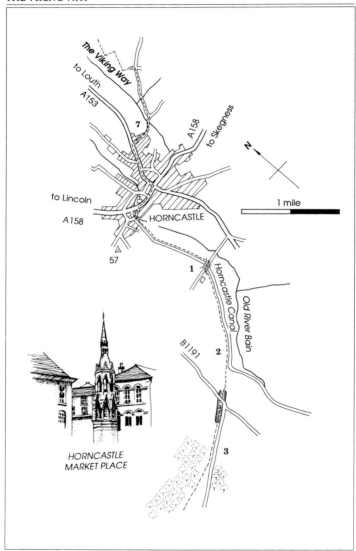

The Viking Way
to Louth
A153
7
A158
to Skegness
N
to Lincoln
A158
1 mile
HORNCASTLE
57
1
Horncastle Canal
Old River Bain
B1191
2
3
HORNCASTLE
MARKET PLACE

The present town has many interesting houses from the Georgian and Victorian eras. On High Street (just off Market Place) is the former town house of Sir Joseph Banks, the famous 18th century explorer, whose other properties included Revesby Abbey, some 5 miles S at the edge of the fens. In the centre of Market Place is a typically Victorian neo-Gothic monument with the profile of the town's former MP, Edward Stanfield.

Just W off Market Place is Bridge Street (leading onto West Street). This is notable for its collection of antique shops and curious little houses, some of which have bowed shop-window fronts dating from the early 19th century. A short distance S is the **Parish Church of St Mary's**, a substantial building of Perpendicular age, with an Early English tower. The latter is topped off with a diminutive steeple.

Inside (on the N aisle wall) is a brass to Sir Lionel Dymoke, a 16th century member of the order of King's Champions, a role which seems to have entailed speaking up for the King at public gatherings. There is also a memorial stone to Sir Ingram Hopton, the Royalist Commander killed at the nearby Battle of Winceby in 1643. Most intriguing is the collection of scyth blades displayed on the S aisle wall: these were possibly used as weapons in the ill-fated Lincolnshire Rising of 1536.

On the S side of the churchyard is the former Workhouse, a white-painted brick building founded in the early 18th century. Next door (and still in use as a dentist's surgery) is the original dispensary dating from 1789, one of the first such houses offering medical assistance to the poor. Round the corner from here is Wharf Road, which runs parallel to the narrow course of the Waring. Half way along is the **public library**, which has on display a reconstructed section of Roman wall, together with exhibits of Roman and medieval pottery (other sections of the old walls are very far to seek). Turning L into North Street you reach the Bull Ring, which has a number of interesting old pubs, including The Red Lion and The King's Head.

Accommodation

The Cross Keys Inn, Salmonby.	Tel: (0658 83) 206
Woody's Top Youth Hostel, for bookings:	Tel: (0205) 68651
The Bull Hotel, Bull Ring, Horncastle.	Tel: (065 82) 3331

The Rodney Hotel, North Street, Horncastle.   Tel: (065 82) 3583
York House, 20 North Street, Horncastle.   Tel: (065 82) 6399

Refreshment
The Blue Bell Inn, Belchford.   Tel: (0658 83) 602
The Red Lion, Bull Ring, Horncastle.   Tel: (065 82) 3338

Camping and Caravan Sites
The Cross Keys Inn, Salmonby.   Tel: (0658 83) 206

Access by Car
To Scamblesby: A153 from Horncastle.
To Horncastle: A158 from Lincoln, A153 from Sleaford.

Access by Public Transport
Bus services Lincoln-Horncastle-Skegness
operated by Lincoln City Transport.   Tel: (0522) 3444
Lincolnshire Road Car Co.   Tel: (0522) 532424

CHAPTER 6
Horncastle to Woodhall Spa

Horncastle - Woodhall Spa (See map p72)   6 miles

The Viking Way leaves Horncastle along West Street, crossing over the by-pass to Langton Hill, and taking the first on the L (a track which leads round to the meeting point of the Bain and Waring rivers). Here you cross over to the E side of the old Horncastle Canal. This was first surveyed in the late 18th century at the behest of Sir Joseph Banks, and opened in 1802 to provide a trading outlet to the Witham south of Tattershall. As such it played a significant role in the development of the town until superceded by the railway in the 1850's.

The Way runs S beside the canal, which has long since ceased to be navigable. Nearby in the E side meadows is the meandering course of the old River Bain. Sometimes these fields also contain a herd of striking white *Charolais* cattle from the nearby farm. After a mile the Way crosses the canal at a road bridge and then joins the trackbed of the old Great Northern Railway line between Horncastle and Woodhall Spa. This section is also known as the *Spa Trail* and information signs provide details of wildlife to be seen along the route.

A short distance along on the R is the brick stump of a former water supply system at Thornton Lodge Farm, originally powered by a wind pump. From here onwards the trail is very obvious along the old railway track, flanked with willows and other young trees. In just over a mile the route swings away from the old canal and enters a shallow cutting before passing under the B1191 (Horncastle-Woodhall Spa) road.

This is certainly one of the most pleasant sections of the Viking Way, passing by the large expanse of woodland on the N side (Highall Wood), which in early summer is carpeted with white-flowered wood anemones. Bird life is also fairly abundant, with willow warblers providing a musical accompaniment. The trail passes a picnic site (with access from the B1191), then an old railway

The Spa Trail between Horncastle and Woodhall Spa

cottage on the L. The scenery is now of lowland heath with typically open glades and stands of mature silver birch.

This section of the route may be cycled, although the trackbed of the railway is fairly bumpy in places. Just over 4 miles from Horncastle you reach the village of Martin Moor, where further progress along the old railway is barred by the golf course up ahead. Instead the Way turns R for 400 yards along a minor road, then takes a footpath signposted L across the N side of the golf course. This is a pleasant route, but you will need to exercise care in crossing the fairways. The path now joins a road passing through wooded parkland and emerging on Coronation Road in Woodhall Spa.

Woodhall Spa (See map p.78)

In 1811 the local landowner, John Parkinson, was prospecting for coal in the area, but instead of coal he discovered mineral water. The water-bearing rocks were discovered at a depth of 511 feet, and subsequent analysis showed traces of bromine and iodine. The health-giving qualities of the water led to the building of the Bath

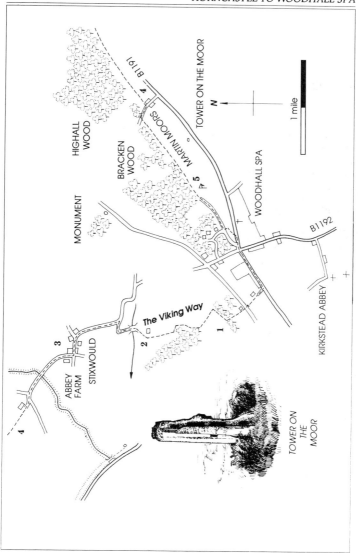

HIGHALL WOOD

B1191

TOWER ON THE MOOR

MARTIN MOORS

BRACKEN WOOD

N

1 mile

4

5

WOODHALL SPA

MONUMENT

B1192

KIRKSTEAD ABBEY

The Viking Way

3

2

1

STIXWOULD

ABBEY FARM

4

TOWER ON THE MOOR

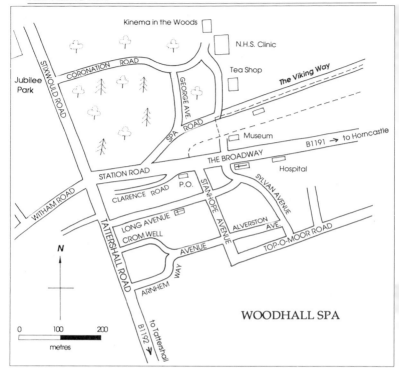

House in 1830, and during the course of the 19th century several hotels and the Alexandra Hospital were added. The popularity of the new spa was boosted by the arrival of the Great Northern Railway in 1855, and henceforth Woodhall became the resort of wealthy clients seeking cures for a variety of ailments, especially rheumatism.

Today the town retains a kind of exclusive charm, although it has long ceased to function as a spa. Its environs are pleasantly wooded, mainly the result of large-scale planting in the 19th century. Most of the shops are found along the main thoroughfare known as the Broadway. Just off this is Coronation Road, a circular wooded drive which leads round to the old spa itself, now occupied by the NHS Rheumatism Clinic.

78

From the outside the building looks slightly decayed, and part of the Pump House is said to have collapsed in 1983. The old steam engine, however, is preserved at the Museum of Lincolnshire Life (see Chapter 8). Next door is the unusual Kinema in the Woods, which apart from showing films has regular summer concerts on the old cinema organ. Returning towards The Broadway you first pass the Tea Shop in the Woods on the L. Just across the Spa Trail is a small **Cottage Museum**, with exhibits based on home life in the Victorian and Edwardian eras. (Open April-September, Saturdays, Sundays, Bank Holidays 2.00pm-5.30pm. Admission free.)

The main crossing point in the town is the junction of roads at the W end of Station Road. Some 200 yards N along Stixwould Road is **Jubilee Park**, a council-owned facility which has tennis courts and an open air swimming pool, plus a caravan/campsite adjacent.

Historic Sites

Further along Stixwould Road, then one mile R along the minor road towards Horncastle, is **Wellington's Monument**. This stands in a grassy field beside the road, and can be reached through a gap in the hedge. Surmounting the monument is a bust of Wellington himself. The inscription records that the oak woodland nearby was:

> "Raised from acorns planted immediately after the memorable Battle of Waterloo."

18th June 1815

One mile E of the town just off the B1191 is a curious ruin known as the **Tower on the Moor**. This is said to be the remains of a 15th century hunting lodge built by Lord Ralph Cromwell (of Tattershall Castle). The redbrick tower is some 45 feet high and once had its own spiral staircase. Unfortunately it now stands on private land next to the golf course and access is difficult.

The older settlement in the district is that of Kirkstead, and the remains of **Kirkstead Abbey** can be seen 1 mile S of Woodhall. Take the B1192 towards Tattershall, turning R after 1 mile at the Abbey Lodge (a public house). Along this lane is Abbey Farm, and a short distance beyond on the L the open field in which stands a lofty fragment of stonework, quite isolated though surrounded by earthworks.

Kirkstead was one of a series of monastic houses built after the Norman Conquest in the great arc of land between the Wolds and the Witham. At this time the area was heavily wooded, but some of the religious orders (the Premonstratensians and Cistercians in particular) were renowned for the conversion of such land for sheep farming. With the effects of the Dissolution and subsequent neglect, little now remains of these houses, although there are other significant fragments at Tupholme and Barlings.

A further 200 yards S along the farm track is the surviving **Church of St Leonard's** (note that the key to the church is kept at Abbey Farm). This is described by Pevsner with some enthusiasm as "a gem of a chapel and one of the finest examples of 13th century architecture in Lincolnshire". From the outside the towerless nave appears unremarkable, with little to suggest such accolades. Inside, however, there is a very early rood screen (possibly 13th century), a Norman font and the remarkable effigy of a knight in armour (dated by Pevsner at no later than 1250). The Early English vaulting has a pleasing simplicity and directly above the altar there is a beautiful carved lamb motif.

Tattershall Castle

Hours of Opening: April-October, 10.30am-6.00pm.
        November-March, 12.00-4.30pm.
        Adults £1:50, children 90p. (1989)

Access by Car: B1192 for 4 miles S of Woodhall Spa,
        adjacent to Tattershall village.

This is well worth a detour; being a formidable redbrick tower contained within a double moat, and one of the finest remaining 15th century castles in England. Now in the care of the National Trust, there is an exhibition centre in the E Gatehouse showing local archaeological finds and the history of the Castle. This began in 1231 with the granting of land to Ralph de Tatershall. The foundations of his original castle can be seen on either side of the present tower.

In the mid 15th century Lord Ralph Cromwell rose to high office as Lord Treasurer and began the construction of the brick tower. This created a demand for millions of locally made bricks, requiring

The 15th Century brick tower of Tattershall Castle

equally vast quantities of wood for firing. The re-built tower was completed in 1448, standing 110 feet high with four battlemented turrets. In spite of its impregnable appearance it was probably designed merely as the principal residence of Cromwell, whose other possessions included houses in Nottinghamshire and Derbyshire.

The ground floor is thought to have been the parlour, and this now contains a great Elizabethan dining table (dating from 1526). The S side entrance has a spiral staircase serving the upper floors, each of which has a large central room and several annexes. Each has a grand fireplace built from Ancaster stone and decorated with carved armorial shields. The windows also have coats of arms in stained glass, covering the entire period of ownership from the 13th century onwards.

On the fifth floor you can stand high amongst the battlements, looking directly down into the moat and the courtyard below. All round are splendid views: nearby the runways of RAF Coningsby and the large gravel pits of Castle Leisure Park, further SE the flat expanse of the fens and to the N the extensive woodlands around Woodhall Spa.

Over the centuries the brickwork has lasted remarkably well, but early in the present century it was Lord Curzon who financed restoration work before handing over the Castle to the National Trust. He also rescued the grand fireplaces (in danger of being shipped to America). The island within the moat provides a pleasant walk to the calling of peacocks - notwithstanding the deafening roar of jet fighters which sometimes take off nearby.

Just opposite the Castle on the E side is the **Collegiate Church of Holy Trinity**. This is a cathedral-sized church of beautiful Ancaster stone, reminiscent in shape of Lincoln Cathedral. It dates from around the same age as the Castle (c. 1440) and has winged angels carved in wood and stone high up on the walls of the nave. One rather undistinguished moment in the history of the church was the 18th century sale of its medieval stained glass to Lord Burghley, leaving the interior cold and draughty for many years. A short distance down the A153 towards Sleaford is the entrance to **Castle Leisure Park**. This has all the ingredients for a family day out including watersports, coarse fishing, horse riding, swimming, restaurants and bars.

Accommodation
Claremont Guest House, 9-11 Witham Road,
Woodhall Spa.   Tel: (0526) 52000
Dower House Hotel, Manor Estate,
Woodhall Spa.   Tel: (0526) 52588
Dunn's Guest House, The Broadway,
Woodhall Spa.   Tel: (0526) 52969
The Golf Hotel, The Broadway,
Woodhall Spa.   Tel: (0526) 53535

Refreshment
The Gamecock, Stanhope Avenue,
Woodhall Spa.   Tel: (0526) 52280
Abbey Lodge, Tattershall Road,
Woodhall Spa.   Tel: (0526) 52538
Tea House in the Woods, Coronation Road,
Woodhall Spa.

Camping and Caravan Sites
Bainland Park, Horncastle Road,
Woodhall Spa.   Tel: (0526) 52903
Jubilee Park, Stixwould Road,
Woodhall Spa.   Tel: (0526) 52448

Access by Car
To Woodhall Spa: B1191 from Horncastle,
 A153/B1192 from Sleaford.

Access by Public Transport
Bus service Horncastle-Woodhall Spa run by
Appleby's Coaches, 23 High Street, Horncastle. Tel: (065 82) 3372

CHAPTER 7

Woodhall Spa to Lincoln

Woodhall Spa to Lincoln 16 miles

Due to the length of this section, it is described in two parts. The first 8 miles to Bardney traverses through the clay lowlands of the Witham Vale, then from there the route follows the river bank alongside the Witham fens. Those walking the whole section will want to press on towards Lincoln, as this offers much interest and a good range of accommodation.

The Viking Way runs through Woodhall Spa and out of the town W along Witham Road. In less than half a mile it sets off to the R into the fields running NW. Presently the track goes through a belt of woodland, then skirts around the E side of a second wood before turning N towards the delapidated redbrick buildings of what used to be Bergamor Farm. Here the Way crosses a stile into the adjacent field (with clear evidence of medieval ridge and furrow ploughing) and heads across to the bridge over Reed's Beck. From this point it continues along a farm track, then follows a minor road into **Stixwould**. This is a quiet village which offers little in the way of distractions.

At the road junction in the village the route turns R, and a few yards further down on the L is the delightful white-painted front of Abbey Farm, a building which dates from the 18th century. As the name suggests, this was the site of a religious house, in this case a Cistercian Nunnery, but there are no visible remains apart from slight earthworks which run in a semi-circle around the farm.

Proceeding N out of the village the road crosses a dyke. Shortly afterwards the Way turns L and then R, following a muddy track towards Horsington Farm. It carries on through the farmyard and heads out once again into the fields, a mixture of crops and pasture land. In these parts the horizons are restricted by the shallow terrain, but now and then you may see the distant ridge line of the Wolds away to the E. The prevailing rural peace is broken only by the occasional loud bang from the crop-scarers, and sometimes the roar

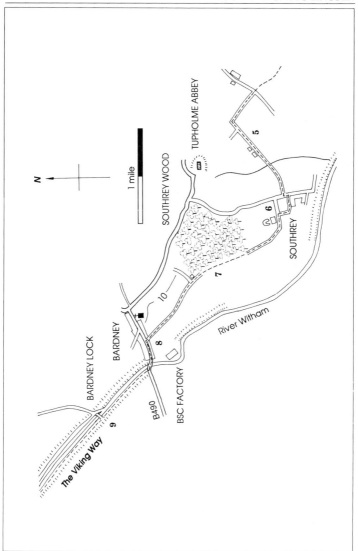

of an RAF jet fighter.

The Way now joins a surfaced lane which presently turns SW towards Abbey Warren Farm. Going past the farm pond is usually quite muddy, but the route then follows a clear track across to the village of **Southrey**. Here a short diversion L leads past the quaint, colonial-looking wooden church and down to the Riverside Inn, with the banks of the Witham just beyond. Remarkably, old railway station platforms are still intact here and the name-sign has not quite been overgrown by the bushes.

The Way itself heads W through the village, passing by an interesting thatched cottage next to the village hall. The road swings around N, and at the next junction the route turns L along a farm track. The farmstead nearby has medieval origins, indicated by the old moat in a pasture on its N side (unfortunately not visible from the track). The route turns NW following a double track, then meanders along beside the dense coppice of Southrey Wood. The foreground is dominated by the view of the sugar beet factory next to Bardney, and before long the track emerges on the main village street.

Bardney

The village of Bardney grew up as an agricultural settlement beside the Witham fens. In the late 18th century the river trade from Lincoln provided a stimulus to development, but in the 1850's this was soon supplanted by the Lincoln-Boston railway. Today the village straddles the B1190 road which crosses the fens and heads off on a devious route to Horncastle. The place is dominated by the sugar beet factory which produces great plumes of white smoke and a rich, not unpleasant smell something like burnt sugar. At one time the factory is said to have had its own narrow gauge railway, but nowadays the beet arrives in lorry and tractor loads direct from the farms.

In the village **St Lawrence's Church** is sturdily built from limestone, and dates from the 15th century with some earlier Norman work. During restoration in 1873 an altar slab was discovered beneath the chancel floor inscribed with seven crosses. This was thought by some to be the burial stone of St Oswald, the sainted 7th century King of Northumbria (of whom more presently). The burial stone was later incorporated within the high altar of the church. A similar stone, said to have been removed from Bardney Abbey, forms part of the altar in the N aisle.

What little remains of **Bardney Abbey** can be reached along a farm track (Abbey Lane) which runs for half a mile N from the village. The remains are in a field adjacent to Abbey Farm, showing the clear outline of grass-covered earthworks. The Abbey was founded in the late 7th century, only to be destroyed in a Danish raid in 870 in which most of the brethren were murdered. In 1087 it was refounded as a Benedictine monastery and remained so until the Dissolution in 1536.

Legend has it that in 675AD Ostryth, the niece of King Oswald, brought her uncle's remains for burial at the Abbey. It being late in the evening the monks refused them entry, despite Oswald's recent elevation to the sainthood. The wrath of God then venged itself as a furious storm blew open the Abbey's doors and a great shaft of light appeared above the saint's body. The God-fearing monks then admitted the body, and for ever afterwards it is said that the Abbey doors were never closed.

About 1¹⁄₂ miles SE of Bardney are the remains of **Tupholme Abbey**, originally founded by the Premonstratensian order in 1160. To get there take the B1190 towards Horncastle, go past Southrey Wood and look out for the remains in the fields to the R of the road. The fragment stands in mysterious isolation and you could almost believe that nothing has changed here in the last eight hundred years. It is, however, in a dangerous condition and restoration work by the Heritage Trust of Lincolnshire proceeds.

The surviving limestone wall was once part of the refectory, and the upper storey has the remains of the Reader's Pulpit (from where the monks were observed during meal times). The wall of a more recent farmhouse stands adjacent, almost propped up by the older remains. Legend tells that the ghost of a headless lady once scared the wits out of a farm labourer guilty of beating his wife!

Bardney to Lincoln   8 miles

Leaving Bardney, cross over the River Witham and follow the path on top of the W side embankment. To the W is the broad expanse of fenland with its black, peaty soils and deep drainage ditches, stretch-

The straight course of the Witham - looking west towards Lincoln

ing away to the Jurassic ridge S of Lincoln. Most of this area is less than 3 metres above sea level, and it contains some of the most fertile soils in the country. The old River Witham once meandered through a flood plain of marshy pools and reed beds, but since the 17th century the Fens have been progressively drained. Apart from isolated farmsteads there is little in the way of human settlement even today.

In less than a mile you reach the junction of the Witham and the South Delph, a drainage channel which runs parallel all the way from Lincoln. There is also the bridge of the former Lincoln-Boston railway. Wayfinding is not too much of a problem as the route continues on top of the flood embankment on the W side of the South Delph. In a further 2 miles the bank swings round to the W, looking directly towards the distant silhouette of Lincoln Cathedral. The ridge line of Lincoln 'cliff' is also apparent, with the Witham Gap where the river cuts through.

Some sections of the channel are flanked with willows and reed beds, a good habitat for summer warblers, herons and other water birds. Across the flat fields you may hear the occasional whirring of

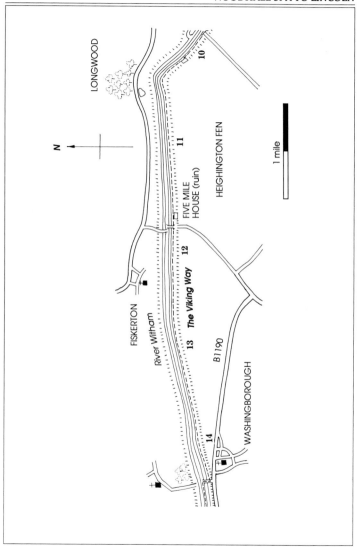

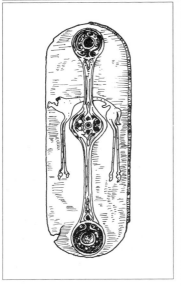

The Witham Shield

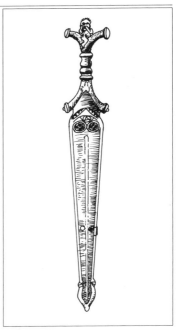

Anthropoid Dagger -
Discovered in the River Witham
in the 18th Century.
Possibly dates from 1st Century AD

partridges in flight. Presently you reach a bridge (a replacement for the earlier chain ferry) which carries a track over to the village of Fiskerton. On the L is the rubble of what used to be **Five Mile House**. Most recently this was a farm, but it once served as a canalside inn for the Witham navigation.

In 1762 the passing of the Witham Drainage Act led to the straightening of the river into its present course. Dredging operations over the next hundred years yielded some of the most significant archaelogical finds in Lincolnshire. These have included the **Fiskerton**

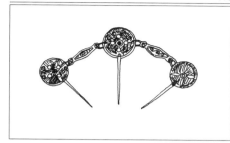

*Fiskerton Triple Pin
8th Century Saxon
Ornament*

Triple Pin, a Saxon ornament from the 8th century discovered here-abouts in 1826. Also buried in the mud were several Bronze Age dug-out canoes, the finest of which is on display in the City and County Museum (see Chapter 8).

Closer to Lincoln the most dramatic find was the **Witham Shield**. This dates back to the Iron Age and is of laminated bronze (originally backed with wood or leather), decorated with three carved boss designs and the outline of a stylised boar motif. The shield is a find of national importance and is currently housed in the British Museum, although the City and County Museum has a good replica.

The last 5 miles into Lincoln is straight, flat and almost endless. The distant outline of the Cathedral acts like a homing beacon, growing very gradually larger (in the opposite direction the Bardney sugar factory provides a similar service). Close to the village of Washing-borough the route crosses the South Delph, next to a house occupying the old railway station. The path now runs alongside the river for the last 2 miles into the city, passing through a belt of outlying factories and emerging on the main thoroughfare of Broadgate.

Accommodation
For Woodhall Spa and Lincoln see Chapters 6 and 8.

Refreshment
The Riverside Inn, Southrey.   Tel: (0526) 398374
The Jolly Sailor, Station Road, Bardney.   Tel: (0526) 398262
The Angel Inn, Wragby Road, Bardney.   Tel: (0526) 398376

Access by Car
To Bardney: B1190 from Lincoln and Horncastle.

Access by Public Transport
Bus service Lincoln-Bardney-Horncastle
(not Sundays or Bank Holidays)
run by Appleby's Coaches.   Tel: (0522) 537799

CHAPTER 8
The City of Lincoln

The City of Lincoln

For centuries Lincoln has been one of the most important cities in the country. In AD 47 the Romans arrived and fortified the town as *Lindum Colonia*. At the time it served as a key junction post on Ermine Street, and at the head of the Fosse Way. Before long it developed into a fully fledged Roman city with a forum and basilica, garrison buildings and villas, surrounded by a complete set of fortified walls.

From the 4th century Lincoln suffered something of a decline, with Roman structures plundered or destroyed by the invading Saxons. A visit by St Paulinus in 627 apparently converted the Saxons to Christianity, and resulted in the building of an early church at St Paul in the Bail. Later with the Danish incursions Lincoln became one of the five boroughs of Danelaw, and it remained under Anglo-Scandinavian control until the Norman Conquest. Despite its importance throughout the medieval period, the poorer parts of Lincoln were said to be in decay until the early 19th century when industrialisation led to a rapid population growth. The city then became famous for its engineering works, producing the first tanks in the Great War.

Today the skyline is still dominated by the graceful towers of the Cathedral which stands opposite Lincoln Castle on the high ground of the 'cliff'. To its credit the city can claim to have preserved the best part of its architectural heritage - through careful planning controls and sensitive redevelopment. As a historic centre it compares well with York or Durham, and accordingly there is a thriving tourist trade.

A Tour of the City

Lincoln easily lends itself to a walking tour, but even a brief visit is likely to take the best part of a day. Starting at the railway station turn L along St Mary Street to the corner of High Street. On the L is the **Church of St Mary le Wigford**, one of the three in the city dating from

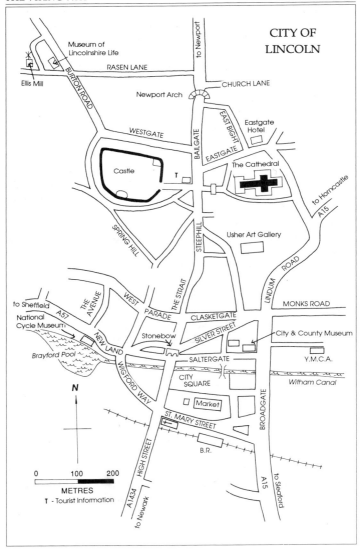

CITY OF
LINCOLN

Museum of
Lincolnshire Life

RASEN LANE

CHURCH LANE

Ellis Mill

to Newport

Newport Arch

Eastgate
Hotel

BURTON ROAD

WESTGATE

BAILGATE

EAST BIGHT

EASTGATE

The Cathedral

Castle

T

to Horncastle
A15

SPRING HILL

STEEPHILL

Usher Art Gallery

LINDUM ROAD

to Sheffield
A57

THE AVENUE

WEST PARADE

THE STRAIT

CLASKETGATE

MONKS ROAD

National
Cycle Museum

NEW LAND

Stonebow

SILVER STREET

City & County Museum

Brayford Pool

WIGFORD WAY

SALTERGATE

Y.M.C.A.

Witham Canal

CITY
SQUARE

BROADGATE

N

Market

ST. MARY STREET

HIGH STREET

B.R.

to Sleaford
A15

0   100   200
METRES
T - Tourist Information

A1434
to Newark

the Anglo-Saxon period. The tower is basically Saxon with corner stones, rubble walls and a restored round arch. On the W face is a curious dedication stone inscribed in Anglo-Saxon, and translated thus:

"Eartig had me built and endowed to the glory of
Christ and St Mary."

Beneath this is a later Latin inscription. Inside the church on the L side of the entrance door there is a stone slab with a carved figure in prayer, dating from the 14th century.

From the church turn R along High Street, the main pedestrianised shopping area. On the R side of the precinct there is a Tourist Information Centre close to the market hall. A further 100 yards down you reach **High Bridge** over the Witham Canal. On the bridge is a 16th century timbered building which now houses the High Bridge Café. A short distance ahead is Saltergate and the early 16th century Guildhall, attractively built from local limestone, which forms the **Stonebow** (or gateway), replacing earlier Roman and medieval gates.

Returning a few paces to High Bridge, you can take a narrow passage to the R of the café, following a path beside the canal. This leads to Brayford Pool which now serves as a marina for barges and pleasure craft. Hereabouts the waters are usually graced by a group of resident mute swans. Brayford Pool is reputed to have given the city its original Celtic name of 'Lindun', meaning pool by the hill. In summer you can take a pleasure cruise through the city or along the Foss Dyke Canal (originally built by the Romans as a connection with the Trent). Further along the quayside a modern redbrick building houses the **National Cycle Museum**. (Open daily 10.00am-5.00pm. Adults 50p, children 25p. [1989])

Retrace your steps beside the canal and emerge once again into High Street, turn L and pass through the Stonebow. Further up on the R are two half-timbered houses from the late 15th century - the Cardinal's Hat and Dernstall House. The former (now the Halifax Building Society) is thought to have been named in honour of Cardinal Wolsey who served briefly as Bishop of Lincoln from 1514 to 1515. Now take the R fork and continue up an attractive cobblestoned street known as The Strait.

On the L is the **Jew's House**, a 12th century stone building with an original Norman round arch above the doorway and similar work above the first floor windows. This was owned by the Jewish community in Lincoln from around 1290. Next door is Jew's Court, which may once have been a synagogue but is now occupied by a bookshop for the Society for Lincolnshire History and Archaeology.

The Strait continues into **Steep Hill**, the naming of which becomes immediately apparent as you climb up the terrific slope. The area is pleasantly populated with cafés, bookshops and antique shops. Near the top is the Harlequin, an antiquarian bookshop within a splendid half-timbered house. Opposite is the Norman House, a limestone building dating from 1170-1180 with a reset round arch above the first floor window. The plaque outside tells us that it is mistakenly known as Aaron's House, after a supposed 12th century inhabitant.

When you finally reach the top at Castlegate, you are in the centre of up-hill Lincoln and at a focal point from which to explore the main historic attractions. To the L is the entrance to the Norman Castle, and to the R Castlegate leads through to the magnificent W front of the Cathedral. On the N side of the square is another **Tourist Information Centre**, within a 16th century timbered house (formerly a National Westminster Bank and currently known as Leigh Pemberton House).

Lincoln Castle

Hours of Opening:
April-October,

Monday-Saturday 9.30am-5.30pm.
Sunday 11.30am-5.30pm.

November-March, Monday -Saturday 9.30am-4.00pm.
Closed on Sunday.

Adults 50p, children 30p. (1989)

Guided tours available.

The Castle was built on the orders of William the Conqueror in 1068, using the base of the old Roman walls. An area of some 6 acres was enclosed within high earthen banks, incorporating two large mounds.

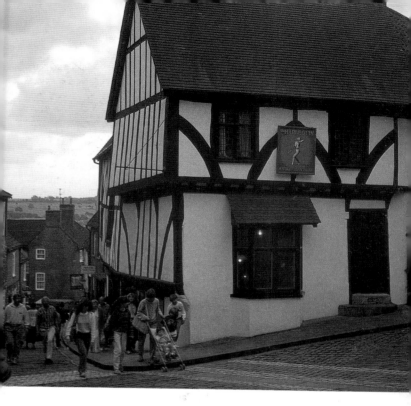

Uphill Lincoln

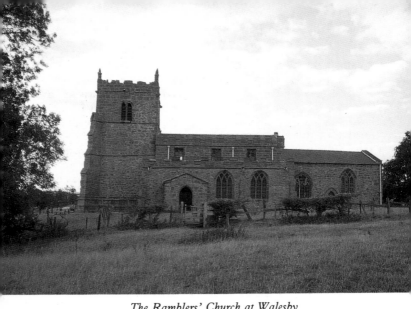

The Ramblers' Church at Walesby

The deserted medieval village of East Wykeham

Later during the 12th and 13th centuries the external walls were completed, forming a formidable fortress in a good defensive position. The Castle was held by King Stephen against Matilda's forces in 1141, and again by Henry III against the Dauphin of France in 1217. After that it fell only once - in 1644 during the Civil War when it was overwhelmed by the Parliamentary army.

The main entrance is through the East Gatehouse, a structure which dates from the 12th century with 19th century alterations. Turn L towards the SE corner of the keep and you can climb the steps to the **Observation Tower**. A narrow spiral staircase then leads to the top of the highest turret. This, oddly enough, was added by a governor of the 19th century prison whose hobby was astronomy! At the top it affords a marvellous view over the whole of Lincoln, and directly across to the high towers of the Cathedral.

Proceeding W within the walls you reach the **Lucy Tower**, a round fortress built on top of the original Norman mound. The short gravestones within record the initials of the prisoners who died (or were executed) during the 19th century. Returning towards the East Gatehouse there is a complex of buildings on your L, with a passageway entrance to the prison chapel. This is remarkable for its high locking pews which kept the prisoners in tiny cubicles, seeing only the priest directly in front of them.

Within the keep there are two 19th century buildings which now accommodate the Lincoln Archives Department and the Crown Court. Perched beneath the walls on the N side is the 19th century **Bath House**, which apparently did have a fireplace for heating the water before the prisoners were immersed! Nearby on the grassy slope is a larger than life bust of George III, which used to adorn the top of Dunston Pillar S of the city. It was removed, we are told, during World War II as a hazard to low-flying aircraft. The walls on the N side provide a high walkway leading to a turret-like building in the NE corner known as **Cobb Hall**. This is said to have been the site of public hangings as recently as the 1850's.

Leaving the Castle proceed back along Castlegate, then turn L into Bailgate. About 50 yards along there are brick setts in the middle of the road, marking the site of the Roman Colonnade which extended for 275 feet. A further 200 yards N is the restored **Newport Arch** (the

*Newport Arch at the head of Bailgate,
the original 4th Century Roman gateway*

original Roman gateway into the city) showing very substantial masonry work. To the R along East Bight there are fragments of the Roman walls which once stood at over 10 feet thick. Along Eastgate (in front of the Eastgate Hotel) it is also possible to view the foundations of a Roman tower, in use as part of the original fortifications from the 1st century AD.

Returning towards Bailgate, turn R and then L into Westgate. A few yards along on the L is the site of **St Paul in the Bail**, which was Lincoln's earliest Christian church. This was built on the site of the Roman Forum and excavations have revealed Roman burials from the 4th century, as well as use by the Anglo-Saxons from the 5th-6th centuries. One of the most significant finds was a 7th century bronze hanging bowl, decorated with bird-like motifs. Westgate continues along the N side of the Castle and into Burton Road where the **Museum of Lincolnshire Life** is situated.

Open Monday-Saturday   10.00am - 5.30pm
　　　Sunday　　　　　　2.00pm - 5.30pm.
　　　Adults 60p, children 30p. [1989]

The west front and twin towers of Lincoln Cathedral

Return once again along Bailgate and turn L at Castlegate into the Cathedral yard.

Lincoln Cathedral

This is one of the finest buildings in Britain and few superlatives can be spared in its description. William Cobbett, not short of an opinion on most matters, was himself almost lost for words when he spied the Gothic masterpiece in 1830:

> "The Cathedral is, I believe, the finest in the world.
> To the task of describing a thousandth part of its
>   striking beauties I am inadequate."

Work on the original Cathedral began in 1072 when Remigius transferred his diocese headquarters from Dorchester on Thames to Lincoln. Disaster then struck with a fire in 1141 and an earthquake in 1185. However, the main phases of building took place in the Early English and Decorated periods (12th-14th centuries), beginning with the designs of Bishop Hugh of Avalon.

The twin towers of the impressive W front stand at 206 feet high. The central doorway has a round arch, elaborately decorated, and above that are the animated figures of twelve English kings from William I to Edward III. Restoration work continues on the W front, funded by voluntary donations.

On entering the Cathedral the first impression is of great spaciousness and height within the nave, which can accommodate up to two thousand people. Next to the S aisle is the solid square font of Tournai marble, with monstrous beasts carved around the outside. Advancing to the front of the nave you can look up to the enormously high arches of the central tower, which on the outside rises to 276 feet. Until 1547 there was a 250 foot spire on top of this, making it at the time perhaps the tallest building in the world.

To the L and R are the main transepts, each with richly decorated stained glass windows. The round window in the N transept is known as the Bishop's Eye. Directly ahead is **St Hugh's Choir**, which was completed before the death of Bishop Hugh in 1200. On the side facing the nave it has stonework of fantastic intricacy. There are two side entrances to the Choir, and from within you can admire the elaborate carving of the wooden canopies. The uppermost stalls are embossed with the names of Lincolnshire parishes, as if reserved for visiting priests.

At the E end of the Cathedral is the 13th century **Angel Choir**, so named after the angels carved in stone high above the great window. The stained glass is modern and shows a myriad of small biblical scenes. The Angel Choir houses the shrine of St Hugh, and the reclining figures of other former bishops. Lincoln is famous for its 'Imp', a curious creature which resides at the base of decorative carving half-way up one of the N side pillars, and is less than 1 foot high.

An exit through the NE transept leads through to the **Cloisters** and the Chapter House. There is also the **Wren Library**, recently restored and containing a collection of medieval manuscripts (including an original copy of the Magna Carta). This description has been rather brief, but first-time visitors to the Cathedral can hardly fail to be impressed.

Those with an insatiable appetite for architecture could now visit the ruins of the **Bishop's Palace**, which are situated off the Minster Yard on the S side of the Cathedral. They include the remains of a 12th century Ceremonial Hall.

Open 1st April-30th September,
　　　　Monday-Saturday　9.30am - 6.30pm,
　　　　Sunday　　　　　　2.00pm - 6.30pm.
　　　　Adults 50p, children 25p. [1989])

The easiest way back to the city centre is via Castlegate and Steep Hill, taking the L fork along Danesgate about half-way down. This leads past the **Usher Art Gallery** which is situated in parkland on the L. The Gallery is in fact more of a museum and is well worth a visit. (Open Monday-Saturday 10.00am-5.30pm, Sunday 2.30pm-5.00pm. Adults 30p, children 15p. [1989]) It contains exhibits of English and Chinese porcelain, grandfather clocks, paintings by the local artist Peter de Wint, and a remarkable collection of coins including Saxon Age coins from the reign of King Edgar (959-975) which were produced at the Stamford mint. There are also Roman and even Iron Age coins. Last but not least is the **Tennyson Room**, containing clothing, clay pipes, photographs and other memorabilia of the Poet Laureate and his family.

Leaving the front entrance of the Usher Gallery proceed down Lindum Road onto Broadgate. Just before Saltergate on the R is the entrance to the **City and County Museum**.

Open Monday-Saturday 10.00am - 5.30pm,
      Sunday   2.30pm - 5.00pm.
      Adults 25p, children 10p. [1989]

This is housed in what remains of a 13th century Franciscan priory. The collections are less compelling than those of the Usher Gallery, but it does contain items of Romano-British pottery, Iron Age and medieval swords from the River Witham and a replica of the Witham shield. There is also Saxon jewellery from the burial ground at Loveden Hill (see Chapter 10). The highlight is a Bronze Age boat, 24 feet long and hewn out of a single oak tree. This was discovered at Fiskerton in 1952.

Tourist Information Centres
9 Castle Hill.   Tel: (0522) 529828
21 Cornhill.   Tel: (0522) 512971

Accommodation
Acorn Guest House, 229-231, Newark Road.   Tel: (0522) 539454
Avon Guest House, 9 Ashlin Grove,
off West Parade.   Tel: (0522) 520674
Bradford Guest House, 67 Monks Road.   Tel: (0522) 523947
The Castle Hotel, Westgate.   Tel: (0522) 538801
The Hillcrest Hotel, 15 Lindum Terrace.   Tel: (0522) 526341
Lincoln YMCA, St Rumbold Street.   Tel: (0522) 528154
Lincoln Youth Hostel, 77 South Park.   Tel: (0522) 522076
Newport Guest House, 26-28 Newport.   Tel: (0522) 528590
Schillings Guest House, 60 Pennell Street.   Tel: (0522) 511329
The Tennyson Hotel, 7 South Park Avenue.   Tel: (0522) 521624
The White Hart Hotel, Bailgate.   Tel: (0522) 526222

Note: complete accommodation lists are available at the Tourist Information Centres.

Refreshment
The Wig and Mitre, Steep Hill.   Tel: (0522) 535190
The Lion and Snake, Bailgate.   Tel: (0522) 523770
The Green Dragon, Broadgate.   Tel: (0522) 524950
The Witch and the Wardrobe,
Waterside North.   Tel: (0522) 538114

Camping and Caravan Sites
Hartsholme Country Park, Skellingthorpe Road, Lincoln.
Open March-October.   Tel: (0522) 568624

Access by Car
A46 from Newark and the A1.
A15 from Sleaford.
A57 from Sheffield.

Access by Public Transport
BR Services to Lincoln Central from Newark,
Sheffield, Grimsby and Sleaford.   Tel: (0522) 539502
National Express Coach Services from
London Victoria (via Newark).

Lincoln Imp - Cathedral

CHAPTER 9

Lincoln to Wellingore

Lincoln - Wellingore   10 miles

This section follows the Jurassic ridgeline of Lincoln 'cliff' above the broad plain of the River Witham. The plateau lands S of Lincoln were once an indeterminate expanse of heathland and gorse, notorious during the coaching days of the 18th century when many travellers lost their way. Today the area is closely cultivated with a criss-cross of roads and fields, but the names of the old heaths are still apparent from the OS map. On the way the route passes through several old and attractive villages and there are fine views W across the low-lands.

Leaving City of Lincoln, follow the main A15 S for half a mile reaching a golf course on the R (the Youth Hostel is 100 yards R down South Park). From here a footpath runs beside the B1188, climbing the slope of the hill. The path then turns SW, running along the crest of the ridge. There are good views back across the City, with the Cathedral prominent on the N side. Towards the NW horizon is the Trent Valley with the cooling towers of three distant power stations.

Presently the Way rejoins the A15, turning L for 50 yards and then R along Coningsby Crescent. Some 50 yards down here the Way is signposted L out into the fields. After 400 yards you approach a complex of buildings on the R (belonging to the North Lincolnshire Health Authority). Here the Way turns R along the farm track (avoid the obvious path ahead behind the houses), swinging around the ridge and turning S.

From here on there are excellent views W across the lowland plain, with fields sweeping down into the valley. In the foreground are the large outlying suburbs of North Hykeham, while the path runs a field's length from the outskirts of Bracebridge Heath. The rough pasture and scrub at the top of the ridge is the haunt of kestrels, sometimes seen hovering against the wind. The Way continues at the edge of the flat-topped plateau heading towards Waddington.

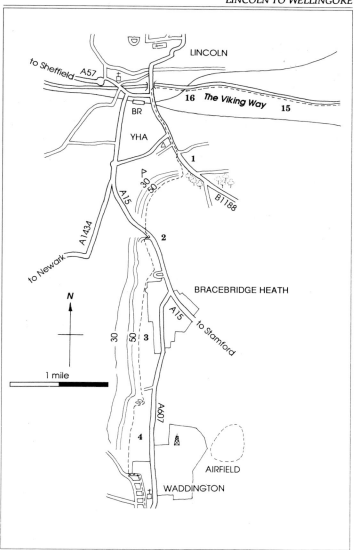

In a further mile the path swings around two artificial ponds before resuming its S course. The Waddington RAF station can be picked out from the radio masts visable to the SE. In due course you reach **Waddington**, a pleasant village with houses of buff-yellow limestone. The Way turns L and then R along the main street, passing the shops and public houses.

At the S end of the village the Way is signposted to Harmston, with the route keeping to the R of the houses and then passing the blackened stump of an old brick windmill. The path is clearly defined, and heads directly for the tower of Harmston church, passing a trig point between the villages. At **Harmston** the Way crosses a meadow on the E side of the village before turning L towards the main road.

A short distance down on the R is the **Parish Church of All Saints**. Its stonework tower is somewhat weathered, but is thought to date from the late Norman period. Just inside the church is the upright stone of a Saxon cross, discovered in the walls of the old manor house. This is remarkably well preserved, with 'woven' style carving and an image of the crucifixion. The reverse side is said to represent the resurrection. The church itself was rebuilt in 1717 by Sir George Thorold, a local worthy who later became Lord Mayor of London. The chancel has marble monuments to Sir George and other local members of this aristocratic family.

To rejoin the Way turn L for 300 yards up to the main road. At the road junction it is sometimes possible to look across to an aircraft parked on the runway of the RAF base. Turn R along the A607, following the path beside the road for just under half a mile. The Way is then signposted R into the fields along a double track. After 300 yards it turns S, heading for the wooded parkland close to Coleby village.

On reaching the edge of the woods you will discover a kind of domed mausoleum half-hidden in the trees. This is known as the **Temple of Romulus and Remus** and was built in 1762 for Thomas Scrope, the owner of Coleby Hall. It can be viewed from a point 50 yards down the track on the R. The interior has an excellent white on blue plaster ceiling.

Coleby Hall itself remains private, although 100 yards further

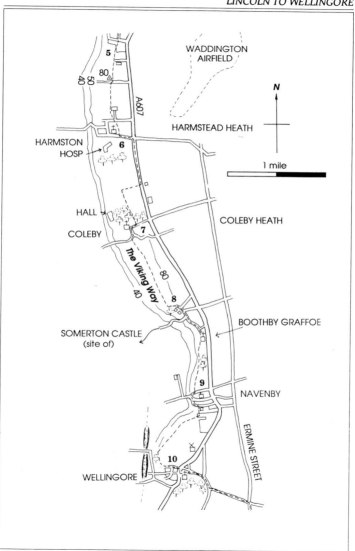

along the Way the 17th century E front is sometimes visible through the trees. Just before the village you pass a rough stonework arch on the R at the entrance to the grounds. The resemblance to the Roman-built Newport Arch in Lincoln is no coincidence - Scrope deliberately chose the design as an imitation.

Coleby is an attractive village, with ivy-clad stone cottages and some houses from the 18th century. It is well within commuting reach of Lincoln, which explains the number of new houses built in traditional stone. Like Harmston and other villages N and S, it sits right on the edge of the limestone plateau, sited close to the springs which issue forth on the scarp face. The parish is shaped transverse to the ridge, originally enclosing an area of plateau (Coleby Heath), the ridge itself and some lowland meadows.

Coleby has a long history, its name indicating its Danish origins. The old Saxon church was rebuilt by none other than Ralph Camerarius de Tancarville, a Norman Lord of the late 12th century. Today Norman work survives in the tower of **All Saints Church**, which is topped off with a slender Perpendicular spire. Inside, the church has architectural styles which bear witness to many alterations over the centuries. The sturdy round pillars of the N aisle are Norman, but those of the S aisle are octagonal and Early English. The square font is also Norman, decorated with interlocking arches. Not to be missed are the grumpy faces on either side of the tower arch!

Round the corner from the church on Far Lane is the Bell Inn. At the end of the cul de sac the village suddenly peters out, revealing marvellous views across the lowland plain. Returning to the church, the Way proceeds S along High Street, passing the Tempest Arms on the R. The path continues at the head of green sloping meadows, passing under the electricity pylons and turning towards Boothby Graffoe. The views now open out, revealing the ridgeline which runs SW below Wellingore. Close to the latter on the S skyline is the tall tower of a disused windmill.

Just before a clump of pine trees the path turns L over a stile, then crosses a short field into **Boothby Graffoe**. Two hundred yards further on a road is signposted R down the hill towards Somerton Castle. This is 2 miles distant amidst the 'Low Fields' close to the River Brant. The present house is a chateau-style private residence which is difficult to see from the road. Very prominent, however, is the high double embankment which formerly enclosed the moat. In 1356 King John of France was held here, awaiting ransom after his capture at Poitiers by the Black Prince. By all accounts the King's confinement did not prevent him from living in some style, with a large retinue that included priests, cooks, minstrels and many other servants.

Back in Boothby Graffoe the Way continues through the village and sets off on a track below the parish church, heading S for Navenby. In early summer the fields below are a colour contrast of green against gold, with cereal crops and the ubiquitous oil-seed rape. The Way rises slightly past a clump of woodland and soon emerges on a side road in **Navenby**. Here the official route turns R down the unsurfaced track to the bottom of the hill (although it is just as easy to turn L onto the main road and head into the centre of the village).

A short distance R off the High Street is St Peter's Church which stands amongst trees at the top of the slope. Proceed down this road to re-join the Way which takes a R fork onto a green lane (quite boggy for the first 100 yards). This turns R going uphill, then R again to head out along a hedgeside at the edge of the plateau. The views are now N, with Boothby Graffoe in the middle distance huddled against the slope. On reaching a stile the path turns SW with a warning to *'Beware of the Bull'*. This sign is not in vain, for a bull has been seen in the field, but usually standing placidly amongst a herd of cows at the base of the slope! The path keeps to the top side of the field and reaches another stile within 300 yards. The views across the lowland plain extend SW to the steeple of Brant Broughton church, some 5 miles distant. Presently the path reaches the corner of a wood and turns L into **Wellingore**.

The path comes out beside the parish playing fields (note the beacon stack with its coat of arms on the L) then turns into West Street and the centre of the village. Here there are old stone dwellings and many prettified cottages, plus the old windmill tower around 150 yards N on the main road. This is the best stopping point before the long walk down Ermine Street, although for a choice of accommodation you may need to return to Lincoln or take the bus S along the

A607 to the villages of Fulbeck or Leadenham. The nearest official campsite is at Hough on the Hill, some 7 miles S by road.

Accommodation

Mrs Mallinson, Old Mill House, High Street, Wellingore.	Tel: (0522)	810634
The George Hotel, High Street, Leadenham.	Tel: (0400)	72251
The Hare and Hounds, The Green, Fulbeck.	Tel: (0400)	72441

Refreshment

The Thorold Arms, High Street, Harmston.	Tel: (0522)	720358
The Bell Inn, Far Lane, Coleby.	Tel: (0522)	810240
The King's Head, High Street, Navenby.	Tel: (0522)	810367
The Red Lion, High Street, Wellingore.	Tel: (0522)	811020

Access by Car
Lincoln - Wellingore on the A607

Access by Public Transport
Bus service Lincoln-Grantham No 601, Lincolnshire Road Car Co (calls at Waddington, Navenby and Wellingore). Tel: (0522) 532424

CHAPTER 10
Wellingore to Carlton Scroop

Wellingore - Carlton Scroop   10 miles

This section runs along the line of ancient Ermine Street for nearly 7 miles before branching off across the fields towards Carlton Scroop. Most of the distance is covered as a green lane, passing through quiet and isolated country, although from Byard's Leap the Way runs beside the B6403. A possible diversion is to continue along this road to the old Roman town of Ancaster.

The Way leaves Wellingore by a L turning just before the neat little church of **All Saints**. This contains the alabaster effigies of a knight and lady, possibly dating from around 1450. Their precise origin is unclear, although the shields on the side of the tomb previously showed the arms of the local Dymoke, Houghton and Disney families. After 300 yards the Way turns R towards Ancaster and then L along the lane signposted to Temple Bruer. This heads off across the top of the plateau, which hereabouts is wide and expansive. Within half a mile you reach the line of Ermine Street, the old Roman road from London to York. The Way turns R to follow the first section, which is a narrow road within broad verges.

So straight in fact is the Roman road, that it runs like a ruled line direct to the next alignment just N of Ancaster. Apart from the forest cover which probably existed in Roman times, there were few physical barriers to overcome for the plateau (at around 250 feet) slopes away very gently to the E. Nowadays in summer you may go past a hazily-swaying field of barley, gently swishing in the breeze. Of comparatively recent origin is the line of World War II gun emplacements on the R of the road, set 150 yards apart and still standing as if in readiness for a German advance from the E coast. They were probably built to protect the wartime airfield nearby.

After 1 mile and the turning to Griffin's Farm, the Way reverts to a green lane which makes for pleasant walking. In early summer this is a haven for wild flowers, especially cowslips which grow in thick

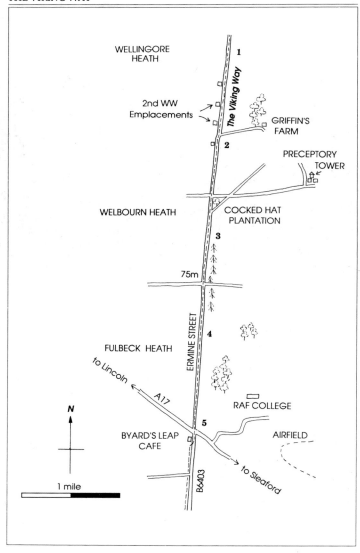

A second world war gun emplacement on Ermine Street

yellow clusters beside the track. In a further half a mile you reach the oddly-named Cocked Hat Plantation. A mile E along the minor road (and well worth the short diversion) is the surviving **Preceptory Tower** of the Church of Knights Templar. This stands between Temple Farm and a rather elegant country house, and can be reached along a public by-way from the road.

The **Order of Knights Templar** was founded in France during the 12th century. This was a kind of cross between a religious cult and a private army, dedicated to the suppression of the heathen, the glory of God and the protection of pilgrims to the holy shrines of Jerusalem. During the reign of King Stephen they founded the Old Temple church in London before moving here to Temple Bruer in 1185. The Monastery - like church was built along the lines of Jerusalem's Holy Sepulchre, amidst lands described as "terra vastata et Brueria" (vast heathland).

The original building had an unusual circular nave, with aisles extending to a presbytery, itself flanked by N and S towers. Just the S tower remains today. In the 14th century the Order was supressed

*The surviving tower at Temple Bruer -
site of a medieval monastery of the Knights Templar*

(some suggest because of the King's jealousy of their heroic deeds) and in 1324 Temple Bruer was transferred to the Knights Hospitallers. Nevertheless, the Order (along with other religious houses) was summarily abolished by Henry VIII in 1541.

The surviving tower has a strange appearance, indeed it even *looks* French (although the wooden pyramidal roof was added during restoration in 1961). Public access is permitted to the interior, the lower floor of which has a vaulted ceiling, wall arcades and a rather indistinct effigy carved in stone. A narrow spiral staircase leads up to the restored second floor. In 1541 Henry VIII and Katherine Howard are said to have stayed here during their tour of Lincolnshire.

Back on the Way the track continues past the wood at Cocked Hat Plantation, with views back NE towards the Preceptory Tower in the distance. Ermine Street begins to undulate for the next mile, but keeps to its direct line, passing a long belt of young forestry on the L. The Way crosses another minor road at Leadenham Heath, and soon the domed tower of Cranwell RAF College becomes visible amongst woodland to the SE. The track itself is sandy with grassy verges flanked by low limestone walls.

Another 1¹/₂ miles brings you to **Byard's Leap** and a crossing point of the busy A17 (Newark-Sleaford) road. Just across on the R is Byard's Leap Café, the first refreshment for many a mile. Here legend tells of the witch called Old Meg who lived with her children in a cottage by the road. Such was her evil spell, spreading pestilence and disease throughout the land, that a soldier from Ancaster resolved to deal with her in person. He rode up to the spot on his horse (called Byard) and, brandishing his sword, challenged the witch to come out. Hearing this threat the witch appeared and promptly dug her nails into the sides of the horse which reared up in fright (hence Byard's Leap). Struggling to keep his balance, the soldier then thrust down and inwards with his sword, running it straight through the witch and killing his own horse at the same time. A likely story I'm sure!

Leaving the scene of this supposed drama, the Way runs as a green track on the R side of the B6403 towards Ancaster. Hereabouts the Roman road is raised up by about 15 feet, befitting its alternative name of **High Dyke**. The surroundings remain as a wide and

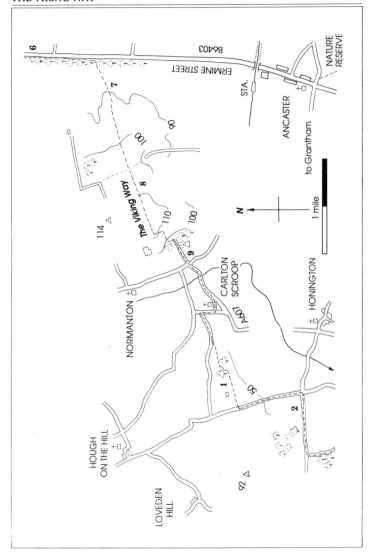

featureless plateau, and it is easy to see how coaching travellers may have lost their way in the past. Despite the proximity of the road the Way becomes a pleasant walk alongside mature trees, passing a public bridleway signposted R in just over a mile and reaching the Viking Way turning some 400 yards further on.

At this point you may choose to head straight on beside the road for the next 1¹/₂ miles into Ancaster, with the possibility of a bus or train into Grantham for an overnight stay. Alternatively there is accommodation to be found in the villages within 3 miles of Carlton Scroop. The Way heads off R beside a field's edge, rising very gradually towards the summit of the plateau. It continues thus for over a mile, passing what seems like an endless series of fields, reaching the crossing point of a bridleway at GR 969464.

The Way now proceeds in similar fashion, heading SW towards a microwave beacon just over the hill and flanked by a tumbledown drystone wall. In a further half a mile the path swings L and R, joining a double track which heads down past the beacon and into the valley. Here you join a footpath beside the A607 for the final 400 yards into **Carlton Scroop**. In the village a faded notice outside St Nicholas's invites you to "rest awhile and enjoy our church". This contains an interesting Norman round arch beneath the tower, and a simple wooden pulpit of Jacobean age.

For accommodation it may be necessary to divert to one of the nearby villages. Of these, **Hough on the Hill** is thoroughly recommended, being 1¹/₂ miles distant along minor roads, and perched on the crest of the Jurassic ridge. Camping is available by enquiry at the post office, with a country inn nearby. Not far away is the **Parish Church of All Saints**, sited next to the mound of an old motte and bailey castle. The main church tower is rebuilt from the late Saxon age, but tacked on the end is a fascinating round turret (with its narrow windows resembling those of a castle). This was possibly the tower of an even earlier church. Inside, All Saints has a high-beamed ceiling, rather like an ornate cruck barn.

A mile SW of Hough is the small hamlet of Gelston, and nearby the site of an early Saxon burial ground with the enchanting name of **Loveden Hill**. In recent years the hill top has been excavated prior to ploughing, revealing 2,000 pre-Christian burials from the 5th century AD *. Most of these were in cremation urns, but a variety of grave goods were also found including glass vessels, ivory, amber beads, bronze bowls and many other items (some of these are on display at the City and County Museum in Lincoln - see Chapter 8). As is so often the case with archaeological sites, there is little to be seen above ground today. It can, however, be approached along the public track running N from Gelston village. The hill has a prominent aspect at the end of the ridge, flanked by a small woodland and seemingly surrounded by the flat lowlands of the Witham plain. Clearly this spot was chosen very carefully by the early Saxon settlers.

Ancaster

The town (nowadays more of a large village) originated as a sizeable Roman encampment close to Ermine Street. Most of the older cottages along the main street are built of the famous Ancaster stone, a cream-coloured limestone which has been used in parts of Lincoln Cathedral and many other public buildings. In the meadow opposite St Martin's Church you can see traces of the old Roman camp, a 9 acre site marked by ridges and uneven ground. Excavations here have revealed Roman coins and pottery, some of which can be seen on display in the Grantham Museum (see Chapter 11).

At the S end of the village is the crossroads of Ermine Street and the A153 between Grantham and Sleaford. A short distance E along Sleaford Road on the R is the entrance to **Ancaster Valley Nature Reserve**, managed by the Lincolnshire and South Humberside Trust. This is a pleasant grassy vale bordered by a long belt of beech woodland. Its flora includes dense patches of cowslips, plus rarities such as pyramidal and fragrant orchids.

Sleaford

This ancient market town lies 5 miles SE of Byard's Leap along the A17, and a similar distance E of Ancaster. It stands at the W extremity of the Lincolnshire fens and its industry has traditional associations with agriculture, signified by the grain maltings on the S side of the town. There are rail connections to Lincoln, Grantham and E towards

---

* See *A Guide to Anglo-Saxon Sites*, Nigel and Mary Kerr, Granada (1982).

Boston and Skegness. On Market Square stands the spired Church of St Denys which contains some fine Decorated window tracery and tombs of the local Carre family.

In the late 17th century the Slea Navigation was opened to provide a trading link with the Witham, and the clear waters of the old cut can be seen as they pass under the road along Southgate. Further down there are several interesting old inns, including the Black Bull which dates from 1689. Meanwhile in Moneys Yard (off the E side of Southgate) there is an old onion-domed windmill lacking its sails, the tower of which can be seen from various corners of the town. Finally at the S end of Southgate, standing awkwardly in the middle of the road, is an early Victorian monument to Henry Handley, a former MP of the town.

Accommodation

Byard's Leap Cottage, Cranwell.	Tel: (0400) 61537
Stonehouse Farm, Newark Lane, Carlton Scroop.	Tel: (0400) 50147
Mrs Bowman, Daisy Cottage, Carlton Scroop. (Non-smokers only)	Tel: (0400) 50523
The Post Office, Hough on the Hill. (B&B)	Tel: (0400) 50229
The Brownlow Arms, Hough on the Hill.	Tel: (0400) 50292
The Red Lion, High Street, Caythorpe.	Tel: (0400) 72632
Woodlands, West Willoughby, nr Ancaster.	Tel: (0400) 30340

Refreshment

Byard's Leap Café, Byard's Leap.	
The Ermine Way, Ermine Street, Ancaster.	Tel: (0400) 30440

Camping Sites

The Post Office, Hough on the Hill.	Tel: (0400) 50229

Access by Car
To Carlton Scroop: A607 from Lincoln.
To Sleaford: A15 from Lincoln.

Access by Public Transport
Bus service Lincoln-Grantham, No 601,
Lincolnshire Road Car Co
 (calls at Caythorpe and Carlton Scroop).   Tel: (0522) 532424
Bus service Sleaford-Grantham, No 609,
Lincolnshire Road Car Co (calls at Ancaster). Tel: (0476) 590111
BR Service Lincoln-Grantham (via Sleaford). Tel: (0522) 539502

CHAPTER 11
Carlton Scroop to Woolsthorpe

Carlton Scroop - Woolsthorpe   14 miles
This is a long section which traverses the lowland plain of the River
Witham, eventually reaching the Grantham Canal near Woolsthorpe.
 It is perhaps fair to say that the scenery is less than compelling,
although there are some pleasant stretches beside the Witham and on
the first part of Sewstern Lane (the old drovers' route N from
Stamford). Some may be tempted to take the bus or train into
Grantham, which has much historic interest and a good range of
accommodation. From Grantham the Viking Way can be resumed by
taking the bus to Woolsthorpe by Belvoir, or by walking the 5 miles
out along the towpath of the Grantham Canal.

From Carlton Scroop the Way proceeds in front of the church,
passing the old Carlton and Normanton National School (now a
private house) on the L, then turns R along the lane signposted to
Hough on the Hill. After 200 yards the route takes a L turn along a
double track heading W. This is followed for less than half a mile as
the Way takes a L fork just before the track starts to rise (the waymark
is not very clear). The footpath follows a line of hedgerow trees up to
a small woodland on top of the hill, skirts the S side of the wood (the
floor of which is often sprinkled with red campion), dips down and
rises up past a slight hollow before becoming well-defined between
growing lines of crops.

On the R you pass the aptly-named Red House as the track heads
on towards the minor road. Turn L here and follow the road as it runs
straight down the slope into the broad valley of the Honington Beck
(a small tributary of the Witham). Here are open views across to the
S slopes of the valley in the vicinity of old Syston Park. A few miles
beyond is Grantham itself, though it remains hidden from here.

Half a mile down the lane you reach a crossroads where the Way
turns R along a farm track. From this point it is just possible to take
a diversion of 1¹/₂ miles up to the old hill fort at **Honington Camp**

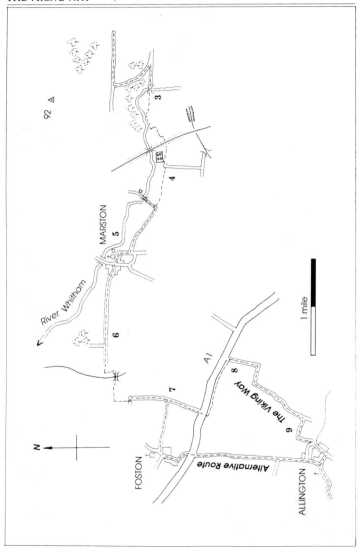

(much easier if you have transport). To get there take the road L for just over half a mile into Honington, cross the A153 and take the rough bridleway which heads up the S slope of the valley, reaching a woodland on the R. Turn R just beyond the wood, then sharp L after 450 yards to the top of the hill.

This is an excellent vantage point, offering views in all directions. Not far away to the SE is the RAF runway at Copper Hill. The fort itself is circular, around 100 yards across and surrounded by double banks and ditches 12 feet deep. Its origin is certainly Iron Age and it compares with some of the best hill forts in the country. There is open access to wander across the ancient earthworks, isolated now within cultivated fields.

Returning to the crossroads on the Barkston-Hough road, the Way proceeds W along the farm track signposted as a 'No Through Road'. The track is followed for half a mile up the rise, where the Way turns L and runs down towards Barkston Gorse Farm (now just a collection of buildings). The route continues down into the valley passing a woodland on the R, soon to arrive at the channel of Honington Beck.

Here the Way doubles back sharp R to approach the bridge over the River Witham which runs as a clear stream winding along through a pleasant wooded valley. For the next 2 miles into Marston, the Way follows the course of the Witham, passing through fields around 200-400 yards from the river. A short distance beyond the bridge the route briefly runs beside the river itself, before turning L and R to pass under the east coast main line railway, now staked out with electrification pylons. From the culvert the track proceeds along the S side of a sewage farm and then out across a lowland meadow.

This meadow is usually grazed by sheep, with the plaintive call of lapwings in the background. At the far end of it the Way takes a narrow lane for the last half mile towards **Marston**, turning R at the junction and following the road round into the village. Being within easy reach of Grantham, Marston has more than a little new housing, with many gentrified redbrick villas. In the centre stands The Thorold Arms, named after a local family of some repute, the Lords of the Manor since the 14th century.

Not far away is the ironstone **Church of St Mary's**. This has a special Thorold Chapel at the head of the S aisle, full of elaborate tombs to successive generations. Marston Old Hall nearby was built by John Thorold in the reign of Henry VII, and later damaged by Cromwellian troops who used it as temporary quarters during the Civil War. Outside the S porch in the churchyard is an interesting 17th century sundial with three faces and, not far away, an ancient laburnum tree thought to be one of the largest in England.

From the centre of the village the route continues W along Stonepit Lane, heading out into flat agricultural lands in the Witham plain. In just over a mile the track reaches the channel of the Foston Beck, turning L and then R to cross the stream at the footbridge. The Way now heads W for 400 yards under the electricity pylons before turning S to join a green lane. Half a mile along here there is a turning R towards Foston, which is clearly visible a short distance away to the W. (Note: the next section takes a very unsatisfactory route beside the A1, so you may choose the alternative via Foston and the minor road to Allington.)

The official route emerges 500 yards further on at the A1 dual carriageway. Here, having made a dash to beat the traffic, you will need to negotiate your way along the broad grassy verge of the main road for the next half mile SE - hardly the best route for a long distance footpath! Before the petrol station look out for an open lane on the R, usually waymarked. This heads off S across the lowland plain and zig-zags its way for the next 1½ miles towards Allington. Away to the SE you can see the Jurassic ridge on the outskirts of Grantham, rising up from the plain like a bevelled edge.

After a mile the Way forks R, rising gradually on a track towards **Allington**. In the village the route turns R and follows the road around before turning R again to emerge by the village cross, not far from The Welby Arms and the post office. Turning S the Way now follows the lane off to the R marked as a 'No Through Road'. A few yards down on the R a set of iron gates mark the entrance to **Holy Trinity Church**, which hides away at the top of the drive.

This is a church in miniature, built of limestone but patched up in brick, it appears at some stage to have lost its tower. Surprisingly, this is of some historic interest with its four Norman round arches in the N aisle and a well-preserved Perpendicular font. The coat of arms on the N wall of the chancel is a dismembered arm clutching a purse,

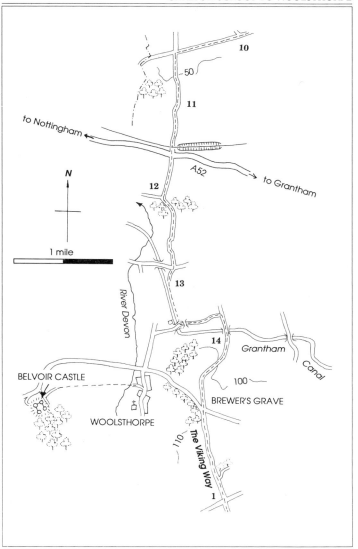

to Nottingham

to Grantham

A52

N

1 mile

River Devon

BELVOIR CASTLE

WOOLSTHORPE

Grantham Canal

BREWER'S GRAVE

The Viking Way

10

11

12

13

14

50

100

110

1

probably representing the local Welby family. According to the church notes, the surviving bells in the bell-cote date right back to the 14th century.

In the past, the job of a church rector appears to have been successfully combined with the vocation of poet. It is therefore fitting that **George Crabbe**, the Suffolk poet (1754-1814), was Rector here for twenty-five years. This is a post he combined with his other living at Muston, and for a time with the appointment as Domestic Chaplain to the Duke of Rutland at Belvoir Castle. During this period he also produced *An Account of the Natural History of the Vale of Belvoir*, published in 1795.

Leaving the church, proceed along the lane from Allington, passing on your L an interesting Dutch-style manor house with curved gable ends. The lane heads off SW along a ridge top, passing under a sentry line of pylons and reaching a crossing point of tracks in just under a mile. Directly ahead you can see the thin finger-like steeple of Bottesford church poking up above the W horizon.

At the crossing point the Way turns L to run almost due S. This is the first section of **Sewstern Lane**, an old coaching and drovers' route which preceeded the Great North Road. Its origins may be prehistoric, as it keeps a fairly direct course right across the plateau lands S of Woolsthorpe and continues N to the present line of the A1 at Long Bennington. In just less than a mile the Way crosses the Nottingham-Grantham railway, and shortly afterwards the main A52. Thereafter it maintains its S course, veering SE after half a mile into a wood. (Note: the track through the woodland is often quite muddy - this can only be avoided by taking the footpath R before the wood towards Muston village, then following the lanes to Woolsthorpe.)

The wood in question is an attractive mixture of deciduous species, but heavy vehicles have cut deep ruts in the track and the ground is quite soft and boggy. Nevertheless, after 300 yards you emerge onto a pleasant green lane which continues half a mile S to the minor road close to the Grantham Canal. Here there is an official Viking Way car park, or rather a lay-by, with information signs on the history of the canal. This was opened in the late 18th century, connecting Grantham with the Trent at Nottingham. Coal and lime were transported to Grantham with agricultural produce heading in the other direction.

At this point you cross over a rather grand stile, built in 1977 as a memorial to John Hedley-Lewis, a former Chairman of Lincolnshire County Council and a prime mover in the creation of the Viking Way. The Way heads S for 200 yards, crossing the line of a disused railway before reaching the canal towpath. This stretch of the path is quite picturesque and offers a pleasant walk for local people. In recent years the Grantham Canal Trust has put a great effort into improving the towpath, although the   current scheme to restore the locks for navigation will require considerable investment.

A short distance along the towpath on the L, a new sign indicates 27$^1/2$ miles from the Trent, the distance across the Vale of Belvoir being somewhat lengthened by the canal's twists and turns. Half a mile down on the R is the Rutland Arms, nicknamed the *Dirty Duck*. Camping is permitted here at the discretion of the landlord, although there is an official site at the Chequer Inn in Woolsthorpe.

The Way now turns L at the canal bridge and follows a track E through the fields for 500 yards, before a R turn leads back to the canal. The route continues over the canal bridge and up a wooded track, heading up for the last mile to the crossroads known as **Brewer's Grave**. This is reputedly the burial site of a brewer from Belvoir Castle who met his untimely fate by drowning in a vat of his own beer! From here the road R leads steeply downhill into Woolsthorpe, whilst the Way itself continues S along Sewstern Lane.

Woolsthorpe by Belvoir

The village lies just inside the Lincolnshire boundary beside the infant stream of the River Devon (pronounced 'Deevon'). This runs N from the village and passes under the Grantham Canal before taking a devious route across to the Trent. In the centre of the village (up a side road on the L) is The Chequer Inn, which offers pub food and is also a listed campsite. Woolsthorpe is also the start of the **Jubilee Way**, a 16 mile footpath which runs SW in the direction of Melton Mowbray, established in the Queen's Jubilee year of 1977 by Leicestershire County Council.

From Woolsthorpe you can follow the first section of the path to

The west front of Belvoir Castle

reach **Belvoir Castle**. This lies 1 mile to the W, standing on a natural promontory overlooking the Vale of Belvoir. From Woolsthorpe turn R along Belvoir Lane, 150 yards before the Parish Church of St James. This leads down into green pastures and across the stream of the Devon. Immediately the Castle is visible high on its vantage point to the W. The footpath continues along the edge of a meadow, following a line of trees (waymarked with the Jubilee Way symbol of a crown and mitre). This approach offers a good opportunity for a long-range photograph. In just over half a mile the route turns L and then R along the minor road to the car park and main entrance.

Belvoir Castle

The Castle features on many tourist itineraries, with many overseas visitors. Unless you happen to visit in a coach party there is a steep climb from the entrance up the wooded drive. The name Belvoir (pronounced 'Beevor') may obviously be derived from the French *'belle voir'*, for good view. The position is certainly magnificent, with the natural advantage of the hill accentuated in the castle mound, and it affords wide views across the low-lying country of the Vale of Belvoir from SW to NE.

The present castle (rebuilt after a fire in 1816) is constructed as a series of towers and turrets in attractive ironstone. This has been the setting for a number of feature films, including such epics as *Little Lord Fauntleroy* and Stephen Spielberg's *Young Sherlock Holmes*. The interior is a veritable treasure trove of paintings, furniture, porcelain and armoury. The paintings themselves are something of an eye-opener, with works by Gainsborough, Reynolds, Rubens, Poussin and Van Dyke. There are many portraits whose subjects include English monarchs over the centuries and successive Dukes and Duchesses of Rutland. The most impressive of these are in the **Grand Dining Room** which is full of old masters, including the original of Henry VIII by Hans Holbein.

The reception rooms retain all the style of gracious living, most striking in the Baroque elegance of the **Elizabeth Saloon**, full of gilt edgings and satin-covered furniture, and the extensive **Drawing Room** which faces out W with a further complement of tapestries and portraits. Also of note are the numerous four-poster bedrooms. The original castle was built by Robert de Todeni, the Norman Lord who was rewarded for his loyalty to William the Conqueror with a grant of land at Belvoir. Remarkably, his original stone coffin was discovered in the castle grounds during restoration work in the present century. It is now displayed in the **Chapel**. Nearby is the effigy of the 13th century Abbot of Newbo, though the Abbey site itself has been obliterated for centuries.

Other rooms house permanent exhibitions, including one dedicated to the 17th/21st Lancers Regiment. Comparatively recent items include a 1907 Renault and a Russian sleigh. Outside in the grounds (amidst the inevitable calling of peacocks) are the **Statue Gardens** which feature 17th century works by Caius Cibber, the Royal Sculptor to Charles II.

Hours of Opening: March-October, every day except Monday and Friday (open Bank Holiday Monday) 11.00am - 6.00pm. Adults £2:60, children £1:50. (1989) Tel: (0476) 870262

Access by Car: A607 from Grantham, then minor
                                  roads from Denton via Woolsthorpe.

Access by Public Transport: Bus service Grantham-Woolsthorpe,
                                  No 605
                                  Lincolnshire Road Car Co
                                  (infrequent). Tel: (0476) 590111

Grantham

With the exception of Lincoln, this is the largest town (population 28,000) encountered close to the route. It lies in a natural hollow in the upper valley of the River Witham, and first gained importance in early Saxon times, though later it remained subservient to the 'five boroughs' of Danelaw. Grantham received a charter from Edward IV in the 15th century, but only in the 18th century did it begin to benefit from its position as a stopping point on the Great North Road.

The Grantham Canal was then opened as a trading outlet to the Trent in the 18th century, and in the 19th century the town upstaged Lincoln by securing its place on the main line of the Great Northern Railway. At this time the light engineering industry developed with the manufacture of steam rollers by Hornsby (and more recently earthmoving equipment by Aveling Barford Ltd). Nowadays the town is by-passed by the A1 but remains a busy crossing point for traffic in all directions.

A Tour of the Town

Starting from the bus station on Wharf Road turn L to the corner of St Peter's Hill, leading on from High Street as the main thoroughfare of the town. Turn L here and 100 yards along on the R is the statue of Sir Isaac Newton, a former pupil of King's School and the town's most famous son. A few paces E across a side road is the **Museum and Tourist Office**.

The museum is well worth a visit, with displays including Neolithic and Bronze Age finds from the district, as well as significant quantities of Roman pottery and coinage. There is a Roman milestone from just N of Ancaster (laid during the reign of Constantine I) and,

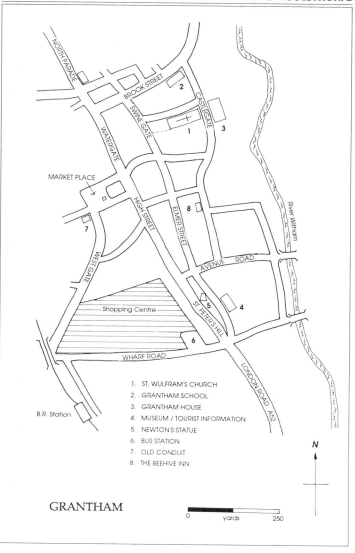

1. ST. WULFRAM'S CHURCH
2. GRANTHAM SCHOOL
3. GRANTHAM HOUSE
4. MUSEUM / TOURIST INFORMATION
5. NEWTON'S STATUE
6. BUS STATION
7. OLD CONDUIT
8. THE BEEHIVE INN

GRANTHAM

0   yards   250

most interesting of all, the *Deae Matres*, a limestone carving of three mother gods from Ancaster churchyard which dates from the pagan post-Roman period. Other themes include the traditional industries of the town (such as leatherworking) and, of course, Sir Isaac Newton.

From the museum head N along High Street through the main shopping area. After 200 yards on the L you reach the brick-built **George Hotel**, the present structure of which dates from the early 19th century. Of its many famous guests, Dickens declared it to be "the very best Inn I have ever put up at" after his visit in 1838. The George is said to have provided inspiration for the inn scenes in *Nicholas Nickleby*. On the opposite side of the road a traditional half-timbered building now houses Catlin's Restaurant.

Around 100 yards further on, High Street joins Watergate with the **Angel and Royal**, the most famous of the town's coaching inns, on the R. This has a 15th century limestone facade and is little changed over the centuries. Its central arch is flanked by worn heads carved to resemble Edward III and Queen Philipa. Like the George it has witnessed many famous guests, including royalty.

A L turn at the Angel and Royal brings you into Market Place. This has a tall column of a market cross, the base of which is medieval. On the S side of the square is an odd stone structure like a mini-fortress. This is the old town **Conduit** which dates from 1597 and has a tribute to its builder, Robert Berymal. Returning to Watergate continue N for 400 yards to the busy junction of the A52 at North Parade. On the R is the former corner shop of **Roberts' Stores**, the birthplace of Margaret Thatcher and one of the town's current claims to fame. This has now been converted into a trendy restaurant known fittingly as The Premier.

Returning along Watergate to High Street, turn L along Vine Street. On the corner with Swinegate is the Blue Boar, an ancient half-timbered inn. The proliferation of pubs with 'blue' in the name reflects a former association with the Whig John Manners, who sought to gain influence by offering free or 'blue ale' at the time of elections. This area also has a concentration of interesting town houses from the 18th and early 19th centuries. Some 50 yards N along Swinegate on the R is the cathedral-sized **Church of St Wulfram's**.

This has a considerable spire, said to be the third highest of any parish church in the country. The present church was begun in the 12th century and owes something to all the main phases of medieval architecture. Quite noteworthy is the Lady Chapel at the head of the S aisle and completed around 1350, the time of the plague. Beneath this it is possible to view the restored crypt from the same period.

However, the most intriguing part of the church (and certainly not to be missed) is the 16th century **Chained Library**, reached by a spiral staircase from the S aisle. This contains the most amazing collection of medieval volumes on the subjects of history, geography, philosophy and religion. There are three hundred books, mainly in Latin (although twenty or so are in English, and many retain their original chains. For this we are indebted to the foresight of the Reverend Francis Trigge, whose Deed of Gift in 1598 provided £100 for the purchase of books for the clergy and parishioners of Grantham.

Pride of place goes to a copy of the *Polyglot Bible*, printed in Antwerp for Phillip II of Spain, with the scriptures in Hebrew, Aramaic, Latin and Greek. No less remarkable is a volume of *Natural History* from the late 16th century, which includes a map of the known world at the time of Christopher Columbus. The map is thought to be identical to the one used on his famous voyage to the New World, showing the East Indies as the first port of call across the Atlantic. Other books include theological tracts for and against the Reformation, and works by Henry More (1614-1687), the philosopher and poet who was born in Grantham. A tour of the library is most interesting and informative (for advance booking Tel: 0476 61342).

At the E side of the church is Castlegate, which proceeds N to the corner of Brook Street with the buildings of **King's School** on the L. This dates from the 15th century and its more distinguished pupils have included William Cecil (Lord Burghley), Henry More and Sir Isaac Newton. Directly opposite the church is the old limestone building of **Grantham House**, dating from the 14th century though much altered since. This is owned by the National Trust but is only open to visitors by prior arrangement with the tenant. Heading S now along Castlegate, after 150 yards you will reach the Beehive Inn on the R. This has an unusual sign in the form of a real beehive outside the pub!

The Beehive pub on Castlegate in Grantham -
note the real beehive in the tree

Before leaving Grantham mention should be made of **Belton House**, a grand 18th century mansion some 3 miles N of the town on the A607. Set within large, landscaped grounds it is described by the National Trust as "the crowning achievement of Restoration country house architecture." It was built in 1688 for Sir James Brownlow and features ceilings by Edward Goudge and wood carvings by Grinling Gibbons, plus a sizeable collection of paintings, furniture, tapestries and porcelain. It also has claims to be the Willingham of Sir Walter Scott's novel *The Heart of Midlothian*.

House and Garden open April-October,
Wednesday-Sunday and Bank Holidays, 1.00pm-5.30pm.
Adults £3:00, children £1:50. [1989]

Tourist Information Centre
St Peter's Hill, Grantham.   Tel: (0476) 66444

Accommodation

Mrs Sharman, Gelston Grange, Marston.	Tel: (0400) 50281
Mrs Cooper, Old Thatched Cottage, Muston.	Tel: (0949) 42880
The King's Hotel, North Parade, Grantham.	Tel: (0476) 590800
The Avenue Hotel, 33 Avenue Road, Grantham.	Tel: (0476) 61876
Archway House, 15 Swinegate, Grantham.	Tel: (0476) 61807
Laburnum House, 35 Gladstone Terrace, Grantham.	Tel: (0476) 66623
Hawthorne's Guest House, 51 Cambridge Street, Grantham.	Tel: (0476) 73644
Lancaster Guest House, 84 Harrowby Road, Grantham.	Tel: (0476) 74169

Note: this is a very small selection of the accommodation available in Grantham. Full lists from the Tourist Office.

Refreshment

The Thorold Arms, Main Street, Marston.	Tel: (0400) 50233
The Malt Shovel, 23 Westgate, Grantham.	Tel: (0476) 63538
The Blue Ram, 11 Westgate, Grantham.	Tel: (0476) 63485
The Black Dog, Watergate, Grantham.	Tel: (0476) 66041

Camping/Caravan Sites

The Coopers Arms, Old North Road, Foston.	Tel: (0400) 81658
The Rutland Arms, Woolsthorpe by Belvoir.	Tel: (0476) 870360
The Chequer Inn, Woolsthorpe by Belvoir.	Tel: (0476) 870250

Access by Car

To Grantham: A1 North and South; A607 from Lincoln.
To Woolsthorpe by Belvoir: A607 SW from Grantham, then minor roads from Denton.

Access by Puplic Transport

To Grantham: BR main line services from London King's Cross; also provincial services from Nottingham and Sleaford.
Tel: (0476) 64135

Bus service Nottingham-Grantham
(calls at Allington, Sedgebrook, Muston and Bottesford)
 operated by Reliance Travel.   Tel: (0476) 64152
Bus service Lincoln-Grantham, No 601
Lincolnshire Road Car Co.   Tel: (0476) 590111
To Woolsthorpe by Belvoir: No 605
 Lincolnshire Road Car Co (infrequent).   Tel: (0476) 590111

The Conduit - Grantham

CHAPTER 12
Woolsthorpe to Sewstern

Woolsthorpe - Sewstern   9 miles

The Way can be resumed at Brewer's Grave, half a mile E of Woolsthorpe up the steep minor road towards Denton. From here the route follows Sewstern Lane as a double track, heading S through quiet wooded country. The first mile is a gentle descent, soon passing over the trackbed of an old ironstone railway (the iron-rich soils hereabouts are deep red in colour) and then crossing a minor road. From this point Sewstern Lane forms the boundary of Leicestershire and Lincolnshire for the next 10 miles S.

Sewstern Lane may have been a prehistoric trackway between the Welland and the Trent, for it runs almost uncannily direct across the low plateau lands of South Kesteven. Its alternative name is The Drift and it still remains in large part a quiet green lane. In the 18th century it was used extensively by cattle drovers to send their herds S to the Midlands and the markets of London. It was also used as a coaching route from Stamford, later to be superseded by the Great North Road. The name 'Kesteven' is said to be derived from the Celtic 'ceto' for wood, and the Scandinavian 'stefna' for district. Nowadays there are still extensive woodlands, but mainly E of the present A1, arising from the proliferation of pheasant shoots and private parklands owned by the landed aristocracy.

From the Denton-Harston road the Lane runs up to the prominent ridge of Jurassic clays. Here the stony surface gives way to a deep rutted track running up through the wood (thankfully less muddy than the wood N of Woolsthorpe). The track emerges on the top of the hill at just over 500 feet, the highest point on the Viking Way S of Lincoln. A short distance further on is the crossing point of the main A607, the busy road from Melton Mowbray to Grantham.

Over the next 2 miles the Way runs as a wide green lane, gently undulating and bordered with bushes and hedgerow trees. In early summer the verges are alive with wild flowers, especially vetches

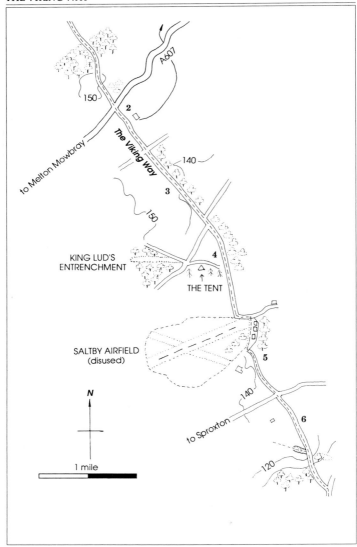

A607

150

2

to Melton Mowbray

The Viking Way

140

3

150

KING LUD'S
ENTRENCHMENT

4

THE TENT

SALTBY AIRFIELD
(disused)

5

N

140

to Sproxton

6

120

1 mile

and cowslips. Reaching the minor road from Saltby there is a wood visible half a mile distant to the SW. This contains the old Saxon earthworks known as **King Lud's Entrenchments**. These run as a double ditch and embankment around 25 feet wide and 10 feet deep, extending for about 500 yards like a miniature version of Offa's Dyke. Their original purpose is shrouded in mystery, although King Lud may have been the late Saxon *Ludeca* who succeeded *Beornwulf* as King of Mercia in 825 AD. Another possibility is that they were built in the latter years of the 9th century to forestall Danish raids from the E. This would explain their plateau-top position facing NE, although how they were supposed to deter the marauding Danes is another matter. (The Danish armies gained full control of the area in 874 with the fall of Mercia.)

The wood itself is marked as private, and the entrenchments quite heavily overgrown. Ironically the same site was chosen for a set of World War II fortifications which stand in ruins close to the road. Nearby, in the wood on the S side of the road, there is also a burial mound known as **The Tent**. This can be reached a short distance along the track heading E and is the legendary burial site of King Lud. It measures some 30 feet across and is now planted with sitka spruce. Once again there is little evidence to declare its real origins.

The Way itself continues as a green lane for another mile, reaching the boundary fence of the former **Saltby Airfield**. Here the Way turns L for 150 yards along a double track, then R across the end of the old runway. Waymarks are conspicuous by their absence, so from the runway head L towards a set of old huts used by the Gliding Club, then R past the more recent hangar. About 100 yards further on the Way turns L, taking a track which starts at a gap in the bushes. This shortly leads on to a resumption of Sewstern Lane, with the steeple of Skillington church visible just over a mile SE.

In just over half a mile the Way reaches a minor road and continues across the plateau turning S. Presently the track of a former ironstone railway heads diagonally across the lane. This originally served quarries in the vicinity of Sproxton and Stainby. Indeed the whole area is scattered with old cuttings and depressions, although their impact on the landscape has been fairly minimal. Sewstern Lane now dips down into a wooded valley before rising up to a crossroads by

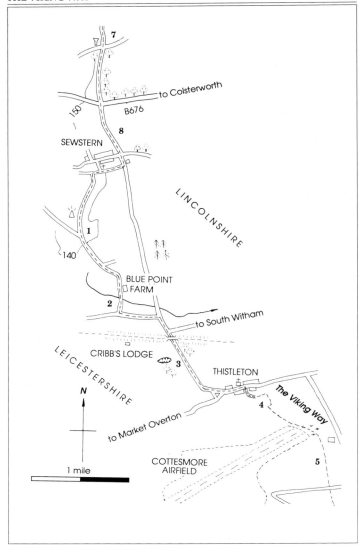

to Colsterworth

B676

SEWSTERN

LINCOLNSHIRE

BLUE POINT
FARM

to South Witham

CRIBB'S LODGE

LEICESTERSHIRE

THISTLETON

The Viking Way

N

to Market Overton

COTTESMORE
AIRFIELD

1 mile

the Buckminster road. Nearby on the R is a concrete water tower with a strange appearance like an upturned funnel.

The Way heads straight on along the grassy verge of the minor road for the last mile into **Sewstern**. This was once a stopping point in the early coaching days but today is just a quiet village, remote even for latter-day commuters. The buildings are composed very largely of grey Rutland limestone in neat regular blocks. Most of the dwellings probably date from no earlier than the 19th century, but with farmhouses directly alongside the Main Street there is a strangely medieval feel. Along here is a Wesleyan chapel of 1903 (now a private house), and not far beyond that is The Blue Dog.

There is accommodation available here, or in the villages of South Witham and Skillington. For those with transport there is the alternative of Thurlby Youth Hostel some 15 miles E, or a visit to Stamford which has a vast range of inns and guest houses. There are two campsites at Great Casterton.

Isaac Newton's Birthplace

This lies some 3 miles NE of Sewstern in the old manor house at Woolsthorpe by Colsterworth (this is not to be confused with the Woolsthorpe near Belvoir Castle). This is an attractive 17th century building, little changed with the passage of time and now owned by the National Trust. The interior is wooden beamed throughout and the ground floor has a very large living room fireplace. There is also well-preserved period furniture and household effects, including pewter mugs.

One of the upstairs rooms explains Newton's early experiments with the spectrum of light. In 1665 he returned here from Cambridge at the time of the plague. For Newton this was "the prime of my age for invention", and he set to work on such diverse problems as binomial theorum, differential calculus and the theory of gravitation. His major work, *Principia Mathematica*, was published somewhat later in 1687 (copies of the book in Latin and English are usually on display). In the manor garden there are apple trees to this day, possibly descended from the one which provided timely inspiration for Newton's thoughts on gravity!

Hours of Opening	April-October, Wednesday to Sunday and Bank Holidays, 1.00pm-5.00pm. Adults £1:50, children 70p. (1989)

Accommodation

The Old Vicarage, Skillington.	Tel: (0476) 860271
Sproxton Lodge, Skillington.	Tel: (0476) 860307
The Blue Dog, Main Street, Sewstern.	Tel: (0476) 860097
Corner Cottage, Water Lane, South Witham.	Tel: (0572) 83258
Thurlby Youth Hostel, Thurlby, nr Bourne.	Tel: (0778) 425588

Refreshment

The Blue Horse, Skillington.	Tel: (0476) 860423
The Tollemache Arms, Buckminster.	Tel: (0476) 860252

Camping/Caravan Sites

Hill Farm, Castle Bytham.	Tel: (0780 81) 229

(No toilet facilities)

Access by Car
To Sewstern: A1 south from Grantham, then B676 from Colsterworth.

Access by Public Transport
Bus service Grantham-South Witham (calls at Colsterworth), Lincolnshire Road Car Co.   Tel: (0476) 590111

CHAPTER 13
Sewstern to Oakham

Sewstern to Oakham (See map p140)   14 miles
For those sturdy souls who have completed the 116 miles from
Barton on Humber, this is the last lap. For those heading N it's the
first. Leaving Sewstern the Way follows lanes and by-ways to Thistleton for the first 3¹/₂ miles, then skirts the E side of Cottesmore
Airfield. It next passes through Greetham and the attractive village
of Exton on its route to Rutland Water. Oakham and the final end of
the Way is then 3 miles along the cyclepath beside the main road.

From Sewstern the Way proceeds S past the post office for 100
yards, taking the first on the R. (Sewstern Lane runs as a minor road
for the next 3 miles, hence the diversion.) Looking R across short
meadows the village Main Street is raised up on a slight ridge,
evidence perhaps of an ancient street pattern. The route continues
past the small ironstone Church of the Holy Trinity and shortly
afterwards is waymarked L along a farm track. At this point the Way
is still 400 feet above sea level, but the countryside appears flat with
isolated trees in large green fields.

Like Sewstern Lane this track has broad grassy verges and is a good
25 yards wide in places. Passing a radio mast on the R, the route is
then joined by a lane from the NE. This is known as Street Lane and
was apparently cut in the 18th century as a more direct route through
to Nottingham. The Way now begins a gentle descent for the next half
a mile, reverting to a single track before Blue Point Farm and then
running up to the minor road from Edmondthorpe.

The Way now follows the road L for 450 yards, then R at the
junction towards Thistleton. At the top of the hill a road sign
proclaims that you are now entering Rutland! The former county
now exists only as a rural district of Leicestershire, having been fully
incorporated since 1974 (though some would be happy to see Rutland revived). On the L of the road is a small patch of woodland
known as the **Thistleton Gap**.

This place was the location of an illegal prize fight in 1811, chosen for its proximity to the boundaries of Lincolnshire, Leicestershire and Rutland. The British Champion, Tom Cribb, faced a challenge from Tom Molineux, a black man from Grantham. A crowd of fifteen thousand is said to have turned up, with distinguished guests including the Marquis of Queensberry. At the end of the fight Tom Cribb was declared the winner, with the victory duly celebrated in Stamford the following Sunday. Cribb's Lodge (half a mile W of the road) is presumably where he lived.

The stretch of road continues for a further half a mile down to **Thistleton**, with the large hangars of RAF Cottesmore visible further S. The village is fairly attractive, although heavy lorries sometimes rumble through on a short cut to the A1. Some 50 yards beyond the church the Way turns R onto a lane heading S. Unfortunately this is not the best section of the route: the footpath through the fields is poorly defined and the Way runs close to the E side of the Cottesmore runways. While this can produce spectacular displays of jet fighters landing and taking off, it can also be *very* noisy.

To avoid this section altogether just follow the roads round from Thistleton to a point half a mile S of Hooby Lodge where the footpath can be resumed. The route itself follows the lane S from Thistleton for 150 yards, and is then waymarked L along a hedgeline for a similar distance. At the corner of the field the footpath turns R to follow the hedge for 400 yards, reaching a signpost before dipping down to cross another field close to the runway (aim to walk in the tractor lines between the crops). When the airfield is active you can often see the jet fighters within 100 yards, throttling up to full power before thundering off down the runway.

The Way continues vaguely across the next field, running directly past a line of landing lights for the airfield. At the far side it is quite common to see a couple of plane spotters materialise out of nowhere. Here, at around 200 yards NW of Hooby Lodge, the Way suddenly becomes well-defined as a double track which leads almost due S for half a mile to the road. The route continues directly across as a track along a field's edge, with the tower of Greetham church visible to the SW. In a further half mile the Way turns R towards a road junction, from which point it then proceeds S along the minor road into **Greetham.**

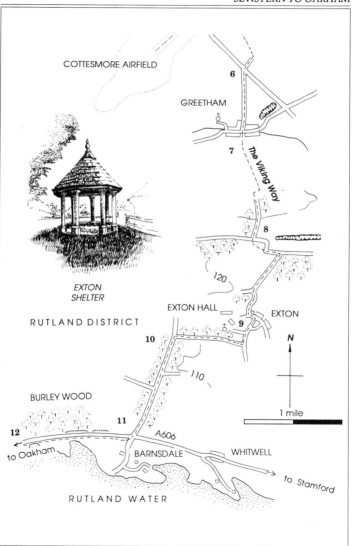

COTTESMORE AIRFIELD

GREETHAM

6

7

The Viking Way

8

120

EXTON HALL

EXTON

9

*EXTON
SHELTER*

R U T L A N D   D I S T R I C T

N

10

110

BURLEY WOOD

1 mile

12

11

A606

to Oakham

BARNSDALE

WHITWELL

to Stamford

R U T L A N D   W A T E R

145

This is a sizeable village built around the busy B608. It has a post office, a village store and, further down on the L, The Plough Inn. Here may be a reasonable place to stop for lunch, being roughly half-way to Oakham. Some 4 miles almost due E of Greetham (or 6 miles along minor roads) is the medieval village site of **Pickworth**. This lies 200 yards W of the present village close to an isolated farmstead. Here the tell tale ridges and hollows are clearly visible from the road. A short track leads up to the farm and a single arch of the medieval church, which is all that remains above ground. Interestingly enough this area has associations with **John Clare** (1793-1864), the farm labourer-poet who lived here briefly in 1820.

Born in the village of Helpston some 4 miles E of Stamford, Clare seemed destined like his parents for a life on the land. Yet his instinctive feel for poetry was remarkable, particularly when it is remembered that his formal schooling ended at the age of twelve. In 1820 his work suddenly came to the attention of the London literary scene, and for a short period he enjoyed fashionable patronage, with a pension provided by the Marquis of Exeter. His *Poems Descriptive of Rural Life and Society* quickly established his reputation, expressing the simple, almost child-like joys of communion with nature. There were also romantic views of rural life, such as an ode to his native village which began:

> "Hail humble Helpstone! where thy valies spread,
> And thy mean village lifts its lowly head,
> Unknown to grandeur and unknown to fame,
> No minstrel boasting to advance thy name,
> Unlettered spot unheard in poet's song,
> Where busting labour drives the hours along."

Clare also addressed the theme of enclosures and the loss of ancient woodland and commons in his beloved homeland:

> "Ye injur'd fields, ye once were gay,
> When Nature's hand displayed
> Long waving rows of willows grey,
> And clumps of hawthorn shade;
> But now, alas your hawthorn bowers
> All desolate we see!

> The spoiler's axe their shade devours,
> And cuts down every tree,
> Not trees alone have owned their force,
> Whole woods beneath them bowed,
> They turned the winding rivulet's course
> And all thy pastures ploughed."

In 1820 Clare married his childhood sweetheart, Martha Turner, and over the course of the next few years they had nine children. Despite reasonable success with his next two volumes, Clare remained extremely poor and slowly began to sink back into obscurity. After the publication of *The Rural Muse* in 1835 he became a voluntary psychiatric patient, and sadly he spent the last twenty-three years of his life in the Northampton asylum.

Back in Greetham the Way restrarts opposite the minor road from Thistleton as a narrow path beside a fence. After 50 yards it crosses a stile and the route opens out onto a double track. This heads off S through the fields, dipping down and rising up beside a belt of newly planted trees on the R. Shortly afterwards there is a stile through a hedge and the Way turns R to join a pleasant avenue of trees, heading into the wooded environs of old Exton Park.

In a shallow valley on the L of the track is an old ironstone cutting. The Way now heads SE across a meadow to rejoin the track at the corner of Tanneley Wood. At this point the Way is signposted R along the open lane (waymarked with the Leicestershire symbol of a Viking helmet and shield). This lane goes past sparse woodland on the L and in just over half a mile reaches the estate village of Exton. Just before the village there is a particularly good example of medieval ridge and furrow ploughing on both sides of the track.

Exton is one of those places which has seen few superficial changes in the last hundred years. In consequence there is a large collection of delightful thatched cottages, and the village is easily the most attractive on the Viking Way. Many of the cottages are built from the local ironstone, with house martins nesting under the eaves in summer. At the first junction there is a pyramid-shaped stone shelter, surrounded by horse chestnuts. Opposite this is St Mary's School, dating from 1874 and now a private house.

Attractive cottages in the village of Exton

Turning R here you proceed along a street of thatched cottages to reach the larger village green, shaded by mature trees with the Fox and Hounds Hotel on the S side. It is worth lingering a short while to see some of the more attractive corners of the village before heading S along Oakham Road. Around 150 yards along here on the R is the entrance to Exton Park. This is a short detour to see the **Parish Church of St Peter and St Paul**. Across the grounds you can glimpse the splendid limestone front of Exton Hall, dating from the early 19th century (with some neo-Tudor designs). In the foreground is the well preserved ruin of the Old Hall, also of warm yellow stone. This, the ancestral home of the Earls of Gainsborough, dates from the early 17th century but was burnt down in 1810.

The steeple of Exton church dates back to the 14th century, but having been fully restored in Victorian times the exterior seems unremarkable. Nevertheless the interior is simply crammed with monuments and historic effigies, reflecting centuries of association with the local aristocracy. Each generation seems to have out-done the last for expense and grandiloquence. The oldest tomb is that of John Harrington (d. 1524) and his wife Alice, both lying at the rear of the S aisle. Then there is the monument to Robert Kelway (d. 1580) in the S transept. This portrays his daughter and son-in-law kneeling beside his body, all suitably attired in Elizabethan finery.

At the rear of the N aisle is the alabaster sculpture of Anne, wife of Lord Bruce of Kinloss, who died in 1627. Here the figure is dressed in a flowing shroud. However pride of place for baroque overstatement must go to the huge monument designed by Grinling Gibbons in 1686, dedicated to the Third Viscount Campden and situated in the N aisle. In this the figures are surmounted by a pedimented arch, and the inscription proclaims the Viscount's loyalty to two English kings (Charles I and II), four wives and nineteen children!

Leaving Exton the Way proceeds S to the first junction, turning R towards Oakham and taking the path beside the road. In less than half a mile you approach a high line of trees known as Barnsdale Avenue. The Way turns L towards Rutland Water, running along the avenue on the green verge. In exactly 1 mile you arrive at the A606 Oakham-Stamford Road which runs along the N side of the reservoir.

Rutland Water

Directly across the main road is the entrance to the **Barnsdale Viewing Area** which has parking, refreshments and a good view of the lake. There is also a so-called Drought Garden, specially cultivated for a low water regime. Rutland Water is claimed to be the largest lowland reservoir in England (which is certainly true), and even the largest artificial lake in Europe (which it most definitely is not). It has developed into a major tourist and leisure attraction with facilities for sailing, trout fishing, cycle hire and nature study. In fact it seems to have everything except a campsite.

The main body of the reservoir fills a shallow valley roughly $2^1/_2$ miles wide by 4 miles long. In the centre is the Hambleton peninsula, joined to the W shore by a narrow isthmus. The reservoir was completed in 1974 and has a surface area of 3,100 acres, serving the water needs of many parts of the East Midlands. The main centre for cycle hire is at the **Whitwell Viewing Area**, 1 mile E of Barnsdale on the A606 (or along the lakeside track). Whitwell also has facilities for own-craft sailing and day permits for boat and bank fishing. For the

Rutland Water, the largest lowland reservoir in England

less energetic there are water cruises on the *Rutland Belle*.

Close to S shore of the lake near the village of Edith Weston is **Normanton church**. This is a distinctive symbol of Rutland Water, having been saved from flooding when the reservoir was filled. It now houses the **Water Museum** which tells the story of the reservoir's construction, with exhibits on local history and archaeology.

> Open April–October 11am–4.00pm,
> weekends and Bank Holidays 11.00am–5.00pm.

Much of the W shore is designated as a nature reserve, managed by the Leicestershire and Rutland County Trust. Some 2 miles further round from Edith Weston is the **Lyndon Hill Visitor Centre** which offers guided walks around the reserve. (Open Easter–October, Tuesday–Thursday and weekends, 10.00am–4.00pm.) It is also possible to visit the Egleton site of the reserve (1¹/₂ miles from Oakham off the A6003) with day permits available at a cost of £1:50. (1989)

Barnsdale to Oakham

The final stretch of the Way runs for 3 miles from the Barnsdale

Viewing Area, following the cyclepath on the S side of the main road. After a mile on the R you pass the estate plantation of Burley Wood, behind which is the grand stately home of Burley on the Hill, visible in a further half mile. The present house was built by the Earl of Nottingham in the late 17th century. Its splendid interior compares well with that of Belvoir Castle, though it remains closed to the public.

Meanwhile, to the S there are views across Rutland Water to the Hambleton peninsula and the western reaches of the lake. Eventually the cyclepath gives way to pavements on the outskirts of Oakham, the historic centre of Rutland. The final end of the route is on High Street, almost exactly 130 miles from Barton upon Humber.

Oakham

The manor of Oakham has existed since late Saxon times, and in the 11th century was acquired by Edith, the widow of Edward the Confessor. After the Norman Conquest it was granted to Walkelin de Ferrers, who is attributed with the building of Oakham Castle around 1180. The first market was recorded in 1249 and, as at

The 11th Century Great Hall of Oakham Castle

Stamford, prosperity increased during the Middle Ages with the wool trade. Oakham became the capital of Rutland, the smallest county in England until it was swallowed up by Leicestershire in 1974. In the 19th century the town avoided industrial development and it remains quite small with a population of just 8,000 today. It is, however, the headquarters of the famous Ruddles Brewery.

A Tour of the Town

The Viking Way enters the town along Stamford Road, turning R along Catmos Street towards the roundabout at the E end of High Street. On the R is the public library, which houses the **Tourist Information Centre**. This has full accommodation lists and details of historic and other attractions in the district. A short distance along High Street on the R is Market Place, with the buildings of **Oakham School** further round on the L.

Oakham School was founded in 1584 by Archdeacon Johnson, along with the other famous school at Uppingham (some 6 miles S by road). The School House dates from the 17th century, but most of the present buildings (including the chapel of 1925) are less than a hundred years old. In front of the school at the end of Market Place is the 17th century **Buttercross**, a large wooden-beamed shelter with a many-sided roof, which adds a certain character to the car park. Returning past the post office look out for narrow lane leading to **Oakham Castle** on the L.

What remains of the castle today is the 12th century hall, which according to Pevsner is the earliest surviving example of its type in England. Its appearance is something like that of a church, the interior having restored round arches with finely carved capitals. An interesting custom dictates that all visiting Lords (including the monarchy) must leave the gift or likeness of a horseshoe. Hence the walls are covered with a great assortment of outsized horseshoes, with many decorated like coats of arms. The castle was previously used as the Council Chamber and still performs a traditional function as the Magistrates' Court.

Open April-October, Tuesday-Saturday and Bank Holidays
10.00am - 1.00pm, 2.00pm - 5.30pm;
Sunday 2.00pm-5.30pm. Admission free.

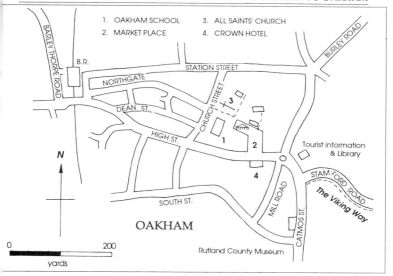

1. OAKHAM SCHOOL
2. MARKET PLACE
3. ALL SAINTS' CHURCH
4. CROWN HOTEL

OAKHAM

Rutland County Museum

Returning to Market Place, turn R once again towards the Butter-cross and take the narrow lane on the R of the school buildings. This leads through to Church Street with the **Parish Church of All Saints** on the R. This has an elegant spire typical of many Rutland churches, dating from the 14th century. Inside the nave arcades are also late Decorated, and each column has carved capitals representing in turn The Fall in the Garden of Eden, grotesque images of the devil and the four evangelists. Others are thought to portray a story from Chaucer's *Nun's Priest's Tale* and even the legend of Reynard the fox.

From the SE corner of the church a walkway leads 150 yards N towards a small parkland, with the **Old Grammar School** on the L. This is one of the original school buildings, dating from the late 16th century and is now converted into the Shakespeare Drama Centre. Meanwhile on the W side of the church and a short distance along Northgate there are some attractive thatched cottages opposite the Wheatsheaf pub.

For those with a little time to spare, the **Rutland County Museum** on Catmos Street is well worth a visit. This houses a vast range of old agricultural tools and machinery, including a number of painted carts, ploughs and tractors. Most interesting of these perhaps is a full size Hornsby threshing machine of around 1890. Another part of the museum has displays of Anglo-Saxon grave goods from two burial sites in the vicinity of Empingham (at the E end of Rutland Water). These include bronze brooches, beads, pottery and iron weapons. Nearby is a section on Whitwell (which itself has yielded Iron Age and Saxon finds) with a photograph of the suspected medieval village site close to the present Viewing Area.

Museum opens Tuesday-Saturday and Bank Holidays
10.00am - 1.00pm, 2.00pm - 5.00pm;
Sundays April-October 2.00pm - 5.00pm.
Admission free.

Tourist Information Centre
The Public Library, Oakham.   Tel: (0572) 2918

Accommodation
Mr and Mrs Brown, Greetham House,
Greetham.   Tel: (0572) 813078
Mrs Wilson, Priestwells, Greetham.   Tel: (0572) 812660
The Fox and Hounds, The Green, Exton.   Tel: (0572) 812403
The Boultons, Catmos Street, Oakham.   Tel: (0572) 2844
The Rutland Angler, Mill Street, Oakham.   Tel: (0572) 55839
Mrs George, 27 Northgate, Oakham.   Tel: (0572) 55057
Mrs Wallace, 11 Market Place, Oakham.   Tel: (0572) 3199

Note: for further details of accommodation in Oakham contact
 the Tourist Information Centre.

Refreshment
The Black Horse, Greetham.   Tel: (0572) 812305
The Noel Arms, Whitwell.   Tel: (0572) 86634
The Crown Hotel, High Street, Oakham.   Tel: (0572) 3631
The Merry Monk, Church Street, Oakham.   Tel: (0572) 2094

Camping/Caravan Sites
Ranksborough Hall, Langham, nr Oakham. Tel: (0572) 2984

Access by Car
To Oakham: A1 South from Grantham, then B668 from
Greetham. A606 from Melton Mowbray.

Access by Public Transport
BR services from Leicester and
Peterborough (via Stamford).   Tel: (0533) 29811
Bus service Greetham-Oakham operated by
Blands of Cotesmore.   Tel: (0572) 812220

The ancient George Hotel and St Martin's, High Street, Stamford

CHAPTER 14
Stamford

Stamford

Stamford is situated 6$^{1}/_{2}$ miles E of the Way at Barnsdale, but having a considerable store of architectural and historic interest it deserves a chapter to itself. The town originated in Roman times as a crossing point of the River Welland, connected along Ermine Street to the garrison town of Great Casterton some 2 miles NW. In the late 9th century it became one of the 'five boroughs' of Danelaw with a township just N of the Welland, and remained under Anglo-Scandinavian control until the Norman Conquest.

Stamford is first mentioned in the Parker Manuscript of the Anglo-Saxon Chronicle in around 918 AD. It soon acquired its own mint employing fifty-two moneyers, second only in importance to that of Lincoln. Stamford Ware (an early form of glazed pottery) became its most distinctive product, and it is perhaps no surprise that examples of this have since been discovered in Sweden.

In the 15th century Stamford aligned itself with the Yorkist cause, only to be seized and burnt by the Lancastrian army under Sir Andrew Trollope. Nevertheless, the expanding wool trade provided a new prosperity, with exports via the Welland to many parts of the continent. Wool merchants such as William Browne contributed to the rebuilding of the town's medieval churches (of which five remain today). Browne's Hospital was also completed in 1475 as a sanctuary for the poor.

Today Stamford is proudly described as 'the best stone town in England', a claim which is probably quite justified if we discount the cathedral cities. There are a remarkable five hundred listed buildings, most of which date from the late Georgian and early Victorian eras. The street pattern itself remains little changed from medieval times, and the consistent use of Lincolnshire limestone creates a visual harmony disturbed only by the modern shopfronts along the High Street.

A Tour of the Town

Stamford is relatively small, but even a brief visit could take the best part of a day. There are five Town Trails (leaflets available from the Museum) with specialist walks to see the Georgian and Victorian buildings. Starting from Red Lion Square (at the W extremity of the old town), **All Saints Church** is prominent on the N side. This has a somewhat worn limestone exterior dating from the 15th century. Inside at the head of the N aisle there are brasses to the merchants Browne and their wives, including William Browne (who died in 1489). The male figures stand on woolpacks as symbols of their trade.

In the NW corner of the church you can stand in a room beneath the tower. Just visible high on the N wall is a curious inscription to would-be bellringers:

> If you that do pretend to ring,
> You undertake a dangerous thing,
> If that a bell you overthrow,
> Two pence must pay before you go." 1694.

William Stukeley, the 18th century historian and famous resident of Stamford, was Vicar of All Saints from 1730-1747.

Leaving the church and crossing the square you can head E along High Street, a pleasant traffic-free zone which has many 19th century facades above the present shops. After 400 yards this continues into St Paul's Street, which has some interesting old cottages on its N side (number 12 has a 17th century facade but dates from medieval times, number 11 has a baker's coat of arms from the early 18th century).

Further up on the L is **Stamford School**, an institution which dates from the 16th century although most of the present buildings are late Victorian. Retrace your steps and turn R into Broad Street, which after a short distance turns itself to head W. Each November from the year 1209 this was used for the traditional sport of bull running, a practice which was finally suppressed in 1839, though not without a good deal of resistance from the locals. Around 100 yards along Broad Street on the L is the **Stamford Museum**, which also houses the **Tourist Information Centre**.

Museum opens May-September,
Monday-Saturday 10.00am-5.00pm.
Adults 25p, children 10p. [1989]

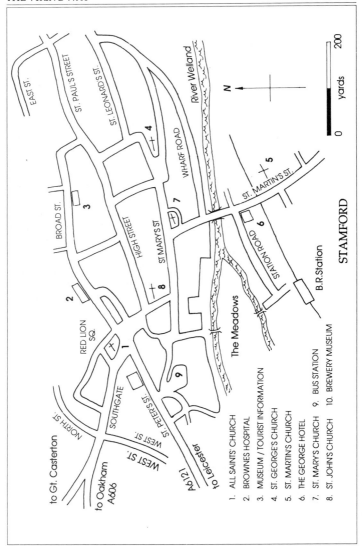

STAMFORD

1. ALL SAINTS' CHURCH
2. BROWNES HOSPITAL
3. MUSEUM / TOURIST INFORMATION
4. ST. GEORGE'S CHURCH
5. ST. MARTIN'S CHURCH
6. THE GEORGE HOTEL
7. ST. MARY'S CHURCH
8. ST. JOHN'S CHURCH
9. BUS STATION
10. BREWERY MUSEUM

The museum has a variety of exhibits including items of Stamford Ware produced in the period 850-1250 AD. There are also coins, in this case silver pennies made at the Stamford mint during the reigns of Aethelred the Unready (978-1016), King Cnut (1016-1035) and Edward the Confessor (1042-1066). Also of interest is the life-size model of Daniel Lambert, the fat man of 52 stone 11 pounds whose only connection with Stamford was that he died here on a visit to the races in 1809. Beside this is the model of the American Charles Stratton, more widely known as General Tom Thumb, who stood just 3 feet 4 inches in height. During the 19th century Stratton actually traded on his size by making personal appearances. After one at Stamford he left a suit of clothing for comparison with Lambert's.

The oldest provincial newspaper in England (and still in existance today) is the *Stamford Mercury*, founded in 1712. The museum has some of the earliest surviving issues on display. Although largely by-passed by the industrial revolution, Stamford did become a centre for the Blackstone Engineering Company, and one of its stationary oil engines is exhibited on the ground floor.

From the museum continue W along Broad Street. Around 150 yards down on the R is **Browne's Hospital**, built in the late 15th century by William Browne, the leading wool merchant of the town. This fulfilled the original function of a 'hospital', acting as alms-houses for the poor. Its present appearance resembling a chapel with a clocktower is partly the result of restoration work by James Fowler in 1870.

Brown's Hospital,
Stamford

A further 100 yards brings you back to Red Lion Square. Directly across, then around 50 yards along All Saints Street on the R is the **Stamford Brewery Museum**.

> Open April-September, Wednesday-Sunday and
> Bank Holiday Mondays, 10.00am - 4.00pm.
> Adults £1:20, children 60p. [1989]

This dates from the early 19th century and operated as a Melbourn's brewery until 1974. It now features all the machinery of a Victorian steam brewery, including an old engine used for serving beer from the barrel. On the opposite side of the street The Millstone (one of the town's many old pubs) proclaims 'Good stabling and loose boxes' on its original 19th century facade.

Returning once again to Red Lion Square, a tour of the S side of the borough begins at **St John's Church** on the corner of High Street. This is very largely 15th century in the Perpendicular style, with a fine wooden rood screen from the same period. The S chapel (next to the chancel) has some excellent examples of medieval stained glass, with other fragments in the windows of the S aisle. Also of note is a brass to the 15th century merchant Nicholas Byldysdon in the centre aisle (usually hidden by the carpet!) St John's has more recent associations with the conductor Sir Malcolm Sargent (1895-1967) who played the organ here as a boy and also sang in the choir.

From St John's head S for 50 yards to the corner of Castle Street. Turn L here and look up towards the steepled **Church of St Mary's**. This is another survivor of the medieval age, with work spanning the 13th-15th centuries. Of special interest are the Early English pointed arches in the S aisle, resting on Perpendicular columns. The N side chapel has painted ceiling panels dating from 1467 and a 14th century limestone figurine in the image of the Virgin. Nearby lies the effigy of the knight Sir David Phillips, a veteran of the battle at Bosworth Field.

Just opposite St Mary's on the N side of the street is a rather grand Regency-style building, the former Stamford Hotel. This dates from around 1810 and is fronted with flamboyant columns. Further along St Mary's Street you go past the 18th century Stamford Theatre on the R to reach the corner of Maiden Lane. Turn R here and then L towards **St George's Church** (which contains more ancient stained glass in the chancel). Here on the S side of Maiden Lane is perhaps the finest Georgian terrace in Stamford.

Retrace your steps to St Mary's and turn L onto St Mary's Hill. This runs down towards the river, passing the town hall of 1779 on the L. Just across the bridge on the R is **Lord Burghley's Hospital** with its line of distinctive Tudor-style chimneys. This was built in 1597 by the then Lord Treasurer of England and inhabitant of Burghley House. A short distance ahead a wooden beam spanning the road proclaims the **George Hotel** on the R. Here the original inn is also attributed to Lord Burghley, using a site previously occupied by the medieval Knights of St John. The present hotel, witness to many a famous guest, dates from the 18th century.

Further up the High Street on the L is the fifth of Stamford's ancient churches, **St Martin's**. This has close associations with the Cecil family, with a collection of monuments in the private Burghley Chapel fit to rival even the baroque extravagence of those at Exton. The E window of the church has 15th and 16th century stained glass (some of which was acquired from the Collegiate Church at Tattershall) and the churchyard has the grave of the fat man, Daniel Lambert. The return to the town centre can be made by turning L at the George Hotel along Station Road, then R across a footbridge to the pleasant meadows beside the Welland.

Stamford has more than its fair share of ancient buildings, but perhaps the oldest is the surviving chapel of **St Leonard's Priory**, which stands half a mile E of the town in a meadow close to the river. This dates from the early 12th century and has well-preserved arches on its W front. However, the grandest property in the district is certainly **Burghley House**, standing in landscaped parkland 1 mile S of Stamford off the B1081.

This famous Elizabethan mansion was built for William Cecil, first Lord Burghley, between 1546-1587. The exterior retains its 16th century appearance, with Elizabethan-style windows and buttresses rising to cupola domes with spires. The inside is sumptuously decorated with paintings and sculpture collected by the 17th century incumbent, John Burghley, fifth Earl of Exeter. Of special merit is the **Heaven Room**, its walls and ceilings painted in fantastic detail, showing a host of semi-clad figures in mid-flight against a background of Graeco-Roman columns. The grounds at Burghley were designed by Capability Brown and are, of course, the setting for the September *horse trails* which attract large numbers of additional visitors.

House opens every day April-October, 11.00am-5.00pm.

Adults £3, children £1:70. [1989]

Information and bookings Tel: (0780) 52451.

Needless to say, the above is just a brief summary of the most interesting buildings in the town. There are many more Georgian terraces and fine 19th century town houses, with much greater detail available in the Town Trail leaflets or (for real architecture buffs) a copy of the Lincolnshire volume in the *Buildings of England* series by Pevsner.

Tourist Information Centre
Broad Street, Stamford.   Tel: (0780) 55611

Accommodation
The Crown Hotel, Red Lion Square.   Tel: (0780) 63136
The Gateway Hotel, 51 Scotgate.   Tel: (0780) 52295
The Lincolnshire Poacher, Broad Street.   Tel: (0780) 64239
Mrs Harvey, 20 Main Street.   Tel: (0780) 63265
Mrs Holden, 54 St Leonard's Street.   Tel: (0780) 53654
Mrs Parrott, 6 Brook Avenue.   Tel: (0780) 52711
Mrs Wade, 10 St Peter's Street.   Tel: (0780) 63900

Note: Stamford has a vast range of accommodation to suit most pockets. Full lists from the Tourist Information Centre.

Refreshment
The Lord Burghley, Broad Street.   Tel: (0780) 63426
The Marsh Harrier, Red Lion Square.   Tel: (0780) 62169
The Millstone, All Saints Street.   Tel: (0780) 62670
The Half Moon, St Paul's Street.   Tel: (0780) 63857
The Bull and Swan, High Street (St Martins). Tel: (0780) 63558

Camping/Caravan Sites
The Taverner Motor Inn, Casterton Hill,
 nr Stamford.   Tel: (0780) 63266

Access by Car
A1 North and South.
A606 from Oakham.
A47 from Leicester.

Access by Public Transport
BR services from Leicester (via Oakham) and
Peterborough.   Tel: (0733) 68181
Bus service Oakham-Stamford (via Whitwell)
operated by Blands of Cottesmore.   Tel: (0572) 812220

CICERONE PRESS BOOKS

Cicerone publish a range of guides to walking and climbing in Britain and other general interest books

LAKE DISTRICT
LAKELAND VILLAGES
WORDSWORTH'S DUDDON REVISITED
REFLECTIONS ON THE LAKES
THE WESTMORLAND HERITAGE WALK
THE HIGH FELLS OF LAKELAND
IN SEARCH OF WESTMORLAND
CONISTON COPPER MINES - A Field Guide
CONISTER COPPER - A History
SCRAMBLES IN THE LAKE DISTRICT
MORE SCRAMBLES IN THE LAKE DISTRICT
WINTER CLIMBS IN THE LAKE DISTRICT
THE REGATTA MEN
LAKELAND - A Taste to Remember. (Recipes)
THE CHRONICLES OF MILNTHORPE
WALKS IN SILVERDALE/ARNSIDE - Area of
Outstanding Natural Beauty
BIRDS OF MORECAMBE BAY
THE EDEN WAY
OUR CUMBRIA
PETTIE (Memories of a Victorian Nursery)

NORTHERN ENGLAND
THE YORKSHIRE DALES
WALKS IN THE YORKSHIRE DALES
LAUGHS ALONG THE PENNINE WAY
(Cartoons)
THE RIBBLE WAY
NORTH YORK MOORS
WALKING THE CLEVELAND WAY AND
MISSING LINK
WALKS ON THE WEST PENNINE MOORS
WALKING NORTHERN RAILWAYS -
Vol.1. East Vol.2. West
BIRDS OF MERSEYSIDE
ROCK CLIMBS IN LANCASHIRE AND THE
NORTH WEST
THE ISLE OF MAN COASTAL PATH
HERITAGE TRAILS IN N.W. ENGLAND
THE LANCASTER CANAL

DERBYSHIRE PEAK DISTRICT
WHITE PEAK WALKS Vol. 1 & 2
HIGH PEAK WALKS
WHITE PEAK WAY
KINDER LOG

WALES
THE RIDGES OF SNOWDONIA
HILL WALKING IN SNOWDONIA
ASCENT OF SNOWDON
WELSH WINTER CLIMBS
MOUNTAIN SUMMITS OF WALES
SNOWDONIA , WHITE WATER, SEA & SURF

WELSH BORDER
ROCK CLIMBS IN THE WEST MIDLANDS

SOUTH & WEST ENGLAND
WALKS IN KENT
THE WEALDWAY & VANGUARD WAY
THE SOUTH DOWNS WAY & DOWNS LINK
WALKING ON DARTMOOR
SOUTH WEST WAY - Vol. 1 & 2
THE COTSWOLD WAY

SCOTLAND
SCRAMBLES IN LOCHABER
SCRAMBLES IN SKYE
THE ISLAND OF RHUM
CAIRNGORMS, WINTER CLIMBS
WINTER CLIMBS BEN NEVIS & GLENCOE
SCOTTISH RAILWAY WALKS
TORRIDON

**CICERONE
PRESS**

Also a full range of guide-books to walking, scrambling, ice-climbing, rock climbing, and other adventurous pursuits in Britain and abroad.

Available from bookshops, outdoor equipment shops or direct (send for price list) from: CICERONE PRESS, 2 POLICE SQUARE, MILNTHORPE, CUMBRIA LA7 7PY

CICERONE GUIDES

Cicerone publish a wide range of reliable guides to walking and climbing in Europe

FRANCE
TOUR OF MONT BLANC
CHAMONIX MONT BLANC - A Walking Guide
TOUR OF THE OISANS: GR54
WALKING THE FRENCH ALPS: GR5
THE CORSICAN HIGH LEVEL ROUTE: GR20
THE WAY OF ST JAMES: GR65
THE PYRENEAN TRAIL: GR10
TOUR OF THE QUEYRAS
ROCK CLIMBS IN THE VERDON

FRANCE / SPAIN
WALKS AND CLIMBS IN THE PYRENEES
ROCK CLIMBS IN THE PYRENEES

SPAIN
WALKS & CLIMBS IN THE PICOS DE EUROPA
WALKING IN MALLORCA
BIRDWATCHING IN MALLORCA
COSTA BLANCA CLIMBS

FRANCE / SWITZERLAND
THE JURA - Walking the High Route and Winter Ski Traverses

SWITZERLAND
WALKS IN THE ENGADINE
THE VALAIS - A Walking Guide
THE ALPINE PASS ROUTE

GERMANY / AUSTRIA
THE KALKALPEN TRAVERSE
KLETTERSTEIG - Scrambles
WALKING IN THE BLACK FOREST
MOUNTAIN WALKING IN AUSTRIA
WALKING IN THE SALZKAMMERGUT
KING LUDWIG WAY

ITALY
ALTA VIA - High Level Walkis in the Dolomites
VIA FERRATA - Scrambles in the Dolomites
ITALIAN ROCK - Selected Rock Climbs in Northern Italy
CLASSIC CLIMBS IN THE DOLOMITES

OTHER AREAS
THE MOUNTAINS OF GREECE - A Walker's Guide
CRETE: Off the beaten track
Treks & Climbs in the mountains of RHUM & PETRA, JORDAN
THE ATLAS MOUNTAINS

GENERAL OUTDOOR BOOKS
LANDSCAPE PHOTOGRAPHY
FIRST AID FOR HILLWALKERS
MOUNTAIN WEATHER
MOUNTAINEERING LITERATURE
SKI THE NORDIC WAY
THE ADVENTURE ALTERNATIVE

CANOEING
SNOWDONIA WILD WATER, SEA & SURF
WILDWATER CANOEING
A CANOEIST'S GUIDE TO NORTHERN ENGLAND (East)

CARTOON BOOKS
ON FOOT & FINGER
ON MORE FEET & FINGERS
LAUGHS ALONG THE PENNINE WAY

Also a full range of guidebooks to walking, scrambling, ice-climbing, rock climbing, and other adventurous pursuits in Britain and abroad

CICERONE

Other guides are constantly being added to the Cicerone List.
Available from bookshops, outdoor equipment shops or direct (send for price list)
from CICERONE, 2 POLICE SQUARE, MILNTHORPE, CUMBRIA, LA7 7PY

Printed in Gt. Britain by
CARNMOR PRINT & DESIGN
95-97 LONDON RD. PRESTON